D0085539

# PR – A Persuasive Industry?

*Also by Trevor Morris and Simon Goldsworthy*

PR for Asia

PR for the New Europe

# PR – A PERSUASIVE INDUSTRY?

## Spin, Public Relations, and the Shaping of the Modern Media

Trevor Morris

and

Simon Goldsworthy

DISCARDED

palgrave
macmillan

BOWLING GREEN STATE
UNIVERSITY LIBRARIES

© Trevor Morris and Simon Goldsworthy 2008

All rights reserved. No reproduction, copy or transmission of this publication may be made without written permission.

No portion of this publication may be reproduced, copied or transmitted save with written permission or in accordance with the provisions of the Copyright, Designs and Patents Act 1988, or under the terms of any licence permitting limited copying issued by the Copyright Licensing Agency, Saffron House, 6-10 Kirby Street, London EC1N 8TS.

Any person who does any unauthorized act in relation to this publication may be liable to criminal prosecution and civil claims for damages.

The authors have asserted their rights to be identified as the authors of this work in accordance with the Copyright, Designs and Patents Act 1988.

First published 2008 by
PALGRAVE MACMILLAN

Palgrave Macmillan in the UK is an imprint of Macmillan Publishers Limited, registered in England, company number 785998, of Houndmills, Basingstoke, Hampshire RG21 6XS.

Palgrave Macmillan in the US is a division of St Martin's Press LLC, 175 Fifth Avenue, New York, NY 10010.

Palgrave Macmillan is the global academic imprint of the above companies and has companies and representatives throughout the world.

Palgrave® and Macmillan® are registered trademarks in the United States, the United Kingdom, Europe and other countries.

ISBN-13: 978–0–230–20584–0
ISBN-10: 0–230–20584–4

This book is printed on paper suitable for recycling and made from fully managed and sustained forest sources. Logging, pulping and manufacturing processes are expected to conform to the environmental regulations of the country of origin.

A catalogue record for this book is available from the British Library.

A catalog record for this book is available from the Library of Congress.

10  9  8  7  6  5  4  3  2  1
17  16  15  14  13  12  11  10  09  08

Printed and bound in China

# Contents

# Contents

# Preface

This book seeks to use a combination of inside knowledge, experience and scholarship to explore the public relations industry. Our starting point will disappoint some people. We believe that PR is not only an inevitable part of the modern world, but also plays a proper and indispensable role within any democracy, free market or open society. PR is not for us inherently – or even usually – evil. On the other hand, we are not in the business of offering comfort to discomfited PR people. PR looks after too many sacred cows and we have set out to slaughter some. We are not seeking to claim that PR is necessarily good, even in one of its modern guises, that of the corporate social responsibility consultant. Successful PR people are not plaster saints, nor do they necessarily exhibit every virtue: they are far more interesting than that.

PR people have represented all kinds of causes and interests, and have done so using all kinds of tactics. Public relations pioneers such as Ivy Lee and Carl Byoir did not suddenly cease to be PR people when they worked for the Nazis, and the works of Edward Bernays – who revelled in the title "Father of PR" – were studied by Dr Goebbels. But, equally, your favourite charity, celebrity, hospital and politician, as well as the innocuous companies you rely on to meet your day-to-day needs, use PR. Mahatma Gandhi, Martin Luther King and Nelson Mandela were all brilliant at public relations: Mandela still is. So, in their own ways, were Hitler, Stalin and Saddam Hussein.

However morally good or bad its practitioners are, as a discipline or industry PR is *a*moral: we see no problem with facing up to that.

What is certain is that in our generation public relations has truly come of age. Newspapers, magazines, TV, radio and on-line media all abound with references to PR people, PR events, PR stunts, PR disasters and, more and more frequently, to "spin". Indeed in politics the word has almost completely taken over from PR. Future historians wanting to describe the politics of our age will need to understand the concept of spin, and come to terms with the role of the omnipresent spin doctors. But PR's sinister profile doesn't stop there. For those exercised about globalization and troubled by the power of big corporations, PR people are seen as the special forces of capitalism. Many in the corporate world would counter that NGOs, charities and other campaigning organizations are themselves adept users of PR techniques: their publicity stunts are certainly a regular feature of the media landscape.

Journalists can seldom resist writing disparagingly about public relations, a faster growing, better paid and better resourced industry than their own. Today PR provides the material for an ever larger part of the content that increasingly pressurized journalists need to produce to satisfy their publics, advertisers and shareholders. As the media has developed new digital forms, PR has quickly responded, exhibiting its power in the blogosphere and in other forms of "citizen journalism". So it is not surprising that journalistic resentment at PR bubbles to the surface: indeed one of the main problems for PR's own image makers is that the journalists usually have the last word.

One motive for writing this book was to offer a PR voice in the one-sided debate in which many journalists lament the difficulties that beset their craft and, after pinning much of the blame on PR, clutch at straws in their search for a solution. They do not want to hear from the adversary they revile, and PR for its part gets on quietly with its work. But PR is here to stay – and grow – and there is no miracle cure for the *travails* of modern journalism. To fail to recognize this is to remain trapped in an intellectual *cul de sac*. We think it behoves a mature PR industry to suggest it may be part of the solution and not just a problem. A large and diverse PR industry may be the most realistic and effective way of putting across the different views and representing the different interests in society. Meanwhile journalists will increasingly play the important but limited role of reporting PR and refereeing PR struggles. This is likely to define the shape of much of the modern media.

Journalism aside, not all popular perceptions of PR are dark and gloomy. Alongside sinister spin doctors and Machiavellian PR gurus exists the world of *Sex and the City*'s Samantha Jones, or of "AbFab", *Absolutely Fabulous*, the hit BBC comedy series. This is the *milieu* of the "PR girl", usually depicted as floating like so much froth on the cappuccino of modern metropolitan life. PR girls do not only exist in fiction. When President Bill Clinton's team wanted to find a job for Monica Lewinsky, the job they looked for was in PR. During the 2004 US presidential race John Kerry was accused of having an affair – with a woman working in PR; and in 2008 similar allegations emerged about Senator John McCain, this time involving a female lobbyist. In Britain not one but two of the Queen's daughters-in-law worked in PR. And when the international football star David Beckham was alleged to have had an extramarital affair with Rebecca Loos, journalists could not agree what she did for a living, but many described her as a "PR girl", thus further imbuing the term with some of the resonances that anyone who googles "PR girl" will find.

These popular images of PR may not seem fine or worthy, but they are far more prevalent in the media and popular culture than the somewhat pompous and pious self-descriptions of official PR as a 'strategic management discipline' concerned with 'mutually beneficial relationships'.

What the dark, the frivolous and the pompous definitions all tend to ignore are the workaday – and often prosaic – realities of PR. They do little if anything to capture the working lives of the majority of PR people who work for unexciting and largely uncontroversial manufacturers and service companies, small regional consultancies, and countless, often obscure, public and voluntary sector organizations. Their work may feature, uncredited, in the media we consume, but they themselves remain little known. Indeed, one of the paradoxes of public relations is that it seldom involves direct relations with the public.

However, reputation is a complex thing. Notwithstanding – or perhaps in part because of – the apparent hi-jacking of PR's public image by popular culture and a handful of high-profile practitioners, PR has been a global success story in recent decades. Organizations of all kinds want to employ more and more PR people, and more and more people want to become PR practitioners. In many countries PR has boomed, growing much faster than the economies concerned, and thriving in an atmosphere of free markets and privatization. In response universities have started to compete with each other to fill PR courses.

Like it or loathe it, PR has become a key ingredient in many of our lives, but surprisingly little serious thought is given to what PR is and what its practitioners do. Glancing, usually disparaging references to PR proliferate, and some scholars feel free to make overarching comments based on scant evidence, but PR remains under-examined and hard to study. The big PR firms remain shadowy, and PR people working within big organizations do not by tradition seek the limelight. If PR is an industry, it is a fragmented and diffuse one, scattered across all parts of the economy and society in thousands of small cells. In both the UK and the US, for example, the largest consultancies employ fewer than 1% of those who work in PR. Similarly even the largest companies have PR departments that rarely have more than a hundred staff and usually many fewer. PR also operates under many aliases – it seems that only a minority of practitioners like calling themselves public relations people – and its border territories with other communications and marketing disciplines are blurred and often disputed. This makes it difficult for outside observers and scholars to get to grips with PR, but also surprisingly hard for those working in PR to know their own business: no one individual has real experience of all the main areas of PR work.

Public relations is a strangely contradictory business. We hope to explain some of those contradictions.

Contact: _morrisgoldsworthy@btinternet.com_
(mailto:morrisgoldsworthy@btinternet.com)

# Acknowledgments

A big thank you to everyone who helped us with this book, including Duncan Burns, Alastair Harris-Cartwright, Robert Blood, Anne Groves, Adrian Wheeler, Marlin Collingwood, Jenny Cain and Jessica Bush.

We would also like to thank the numerous people, ranging from students to senior journalists, industry gurus and writers, who have stimulated our thinking. As ever, *PR Week* has been an invaluable source of information. We must single out two books and their authors. The first is *The Image Merchants: The Fabulous World of Public Relations* by Irwin Ross. Though written 50 years ago it is still a remarkably accurate anthropology of PR – notwithstanding major improvements in attitudes towards differences in gender and ethnicity since it was written. Even today one can imagine the larger-than-life characters he describes enjoying lunch in any of the restaurants around the world that are propped up by PR expense accounts. Ross demonstrates that the biggest issues that confront PR people are timeless. The second is *Advertising: The Uneasy Persuasion* by Michael Schudson. Written in 1984, it is a perceptive account of PR's elder cousin. Both books have more than withstood the test of time. We will be delighted if our book survives for half as long.

Simon Goldsworthy wishes to thank the editors of a number of academic journals for allowing him to adapt material from articles he originally wrote for them. These include *Ethical Space: The International Journal of Communication Ethics*;[1] *The Media Education Journal*;[2] *La Revue LISA*;[3] and *Symbolism: An International Annual of Critical Aesthetics*.[4]

We are grateful to Vesna Goldsworthy for helping to edit the text and to Alja Kranjec for her work on the index.

All flaws are the handiwork of the authors and no-one else.

Finally, we want to thank everyone at Palgrave Macmillan, especially Stephen Rutt and Alexandra Dawe, who helped make this book a reality.

**NOTE**: Statistics and other data about the PR industry have to be treated with caution. The industry is loosely defined and widely dispersed. As we shall see, anyone can say they work in PR but many – perhaps most – of the people who do use other job titles. No organization can claim to represent more than a small proportion of all of those who work in the industry. Moreover survey findings have to be treated with caution as they are usually based on a self-selecting group who are willing and able to answer survey questions.

A final qualification. Describing the PR industry, and particularly the consultancy sector, is like charting shifting sands. Names and ownership are constantly changing. Anyone needing up-to-the-minute details should go on-line.

# CHAPTER 1

# The allure of PR

## Parties, power and postmodernism!

If you are a parent reading this book, particularly (it has to be said) of a daughter, it is quite likely that your child will consider a career in PR. Public relations is now a hugely popular career. For university graduates in the United Kingdom it has come third, after journalism and teaching, as a career choice.[1] Large numbers of PR courses have emerged to try to cater for this demand, which has become truly global. Many more people seek to break into PR after starting their careers elsewhere. Above all, switching to PR has become an escape route for journalists. And as the PR industry continues to surge ahead, faster than the economy in many countries – it has been suggested that the *annual* growth rate in PR is over 30% in China,[2] up to 40% in Russia,[3] and up to 60% in Turkey[4] – this becomes more, not less, likely.

This international phenomenon bears some examination. Why does PR exert this fascination?

One starting point is the interviews the authors have conducted with countless applicants for undergraduate and postgraduate courses from many countries. They are revealing, and confirm that the PR industry, though seen as glamorous, is surprisingly anonymous. Few can name more than one or two well-known PR practitioners – if that. The names of even the largest PR consultancies are usually unknown. Most people have difficulty identifying PR campaigns, and, when they try, they frequently confuse them with advertising and other forms of marketing. Few are aware of PR's trade publications or have visited the websites of its trade bodies. If they have studied the media at school or college they tend to have barely touched on PR. In terms of real-life names, faces, facts, and figures – even concepts – PR is largely a blank.

Nor do many of those interested in PR careers have direct experience or knowledge of PR in the way that is often the case for many other careers. After all, students and graduates who are interested in teaching careers will have seen many teachers at work, and would-be journalists will have seen journalists reporting on television, or will have read their output in newspapers or magazines. They, or their families, are likely to have had direct dealings with people in many other popular careers. They will know – professionally if not socially – doctors, dentists, retailers, people working in financial services, and perhaps lawyers too.

Not so with PR. PR people do not offer a direct service to the public in the way that many other occupations do. Instead they serve organizations, or sometimes rich or powerful individuals, and in the main operate indirectly, through the mass media and by other means. As the numbers of people working in PR grow people are more likely to know someone in the field, but the numbers are still not huge and so the chances of direct contact are relatively low. In the United States, the home of the world's largest PR industry, there are, according to the Department of Labor, perhaps 240,000 people in PR.[5] In the UK, by far the biggest center of PR activity outside America, there are fewer than 50,000 people in PR.[6] In most countries the number of PR people is in three or four digits – if that – and by contrast there are many more teachers, accountants, lawyers, and doctors. Moreover, the figures for the PR industry tend to represent nearly all those working in the field, whereas the social footprint of other occupations with their large numbers of related support staff is often much greater: even if one does not know a teacher or doctor it is hard not to know someone working in education or the health sector. The relatively small numbers of PR people are also disproportionately concentrated in major urban centers, further isolating them from the wider public.

If PR is often anonymous and seldom part of people's day-to-day lives, what drives so many people to seek PR careers? Since direct experience of PR is limited, the influence must be indirect. This leads us to the aura surrounding PR, which has enabled it to exert a pulling power that transcends mundane facts and figures and first-hand knowledge of the industry. In many countries PR has a high profile in the media, where the handful of real-life PRs who are well-known break surface; and it is particularly prominent in popular culture, where fictional characters exert immense influence on the image of PR.

*"Scumbags." "Insensitive, manipulative charlatans."*
*"Sleazy ... disingenuous."*

The above words are from a media evaluation company's report into UK newspaper coverage of the PR industry.[7] Journalists' public antipathy toward PR is clear, and is supported by the rest of the report's findings, which showed that only 9% of articles contained positive mentions, and that the position was actually getting worse. Nor is this unique to the United Kingdom, although surveys also show that most journalists are not highly regarded by the public. In the United States PR people are sometimes labeled as "flacks" and disdained by journalists for their attempts to promote stories, although the American relationship is probably more nuanced.[8] Notwithstanding the ideals which underpin US journalism, the commercial realities upon which so much of PR is based are more fully accepted in the United States. It can also be argued that the exclusion of advertising from a large section of the British media (namely all the BBC's domestic television, radio channels, and its website) and the ban on all broadcast political advertising, alongside a fiercely competitive and partisan national newspaper press, has placed a greater premium on PR in the United Kingdom and that this may have aroused more resentment. Even so, the way PR is portrayed in the media often seems far from flattering. Research by Julie Henderson in the United States found that 83% of media references to PR were negative and only 7% positive.[9]

Despite a continuing tradition of public hostility toward PR people on the part of many journalists, and despite the fact that this is ordinary peoples' main source of information about PR, PR's attraction as a career choice remains and grows. Among those attracted are countless journalists, for whom a lucrative second career in PR often beckons.

At the same time fictional characters with PR jobs have swept the world and have become international icons. They range from *Sex and the City*'s Samantha Jones to Bridget Jones and *Absolutely Fabulous*'s Edina Monsoon, and spill over into real life in programs such as MTV's reality series *PoweR Girls*. They often do things that many PR people find embarrassing and demeaning. Complainers within PR want their industry to be taken seriously and resent the way it is often satirized, without realizing that successful satire must have some basis in fact. Although the satirists and others undoubtedly have their own prejudices, they have often worked as journalists or in the media: their knowledge of PR cannot be altogether gainsaid. As the original producer of *AbFab* has explained,

> At least when we started, maybe not now, they were written out of hate really, maybe not hate, anger cer-tainly … A … way of Jennifer [Saunders] letting off steam and looking at all these terrible people in fashion and PR and now it's kind of taken over the world because it seems now that the world is fashion and celebrity mad … worrying and a note on the decline of western civilization.[10]

However PR usually has the last laugh. Samantha Jones of *Sex and the City* has been a highly effective international ambassador for PR, with a reach far greater than that of any PR organization: indeed plenty of PR students, male and female, have told the authors they were drawn to PR by her example. As the producer of *AbFab* put it, despite the rage which originally informed the series when they were shown in Comedy Central in the United States, a body of viewers developed a sense that there was a lifestyle called "fabulous" and that the series showed how you should live your life.[11]

"Official" PR – PR organizations, writers of PR textbooks and PR educators – frequently decry these representations of their occupation. A former President of the UK's Institute of Public Relations, Europe's largest PR trade body, said that "industry needs to move away from its *AbFab* image,"[12] while another well-known PR practitioner said her "teeth were grinding with irritation" when she picked up a popular novel about the world of PR.[13] Indeed the attempts of some PR figures to stress the seriousness and strategic character of their work, and their role within management, represents a reaction to these portrayals of PR. This reaction may seem reasonable at first glance, but for an industry which often says it specializes in reputa-tion management it reveals a remarkable misunderstanding of the subtleties of what constitutes "reputation." It ignores the way reputation is nuanced and multifaceted; how the same thing can be seen in very different ways by different people at different times; and how work which is safe and respectable can also be seen as predictable and dull, while occupations that are riskier and less respectable can also be seen as exciting and fun.

PR is depicted in two principal and contrasting ways in popular culture. We have encountered the first. It is overwhelmingly female, the world of "PR girls": *Sex and the City, AbFab,* or indeed the 1980s Chinese television series *Miss PR,*[14] which featured a group of young and pretty girls working as "Miss PR" in a hotel, and the Hong Kong film *PR Girls,* about hostesses. Here any PR activity is lightweight, perhaps for clubs, restaurants, and fashion brands, but morphs seamlessly into a world of hospitality. The work may at times seem trivial but is also varied and fun.

The second – overwhelmingly male – is the world of the "spin doctors", working for political parties, governments, large companies, or powerful commercial interests: the PR man helping to cover up problems in the nuclear industry in the film *The China Syndrome;* inventing a war for political gain in the movie *Wag the Dog;* defending the seemingly indefensible in *Thank You for Smoking;* or dealing with day-to-day political life in *Spin City.* These days almost any political or corporate-based film or television drama would seem incomplete without a spin doctor. Much more is at stake than is the case in the world of PR girls, and the PR activity is often Machiavellian. Spin doctors are shown wielding considerable power over the fates of people and organizations and are very much at the center of things. Indeed a surprising number of such portrayals of "spin" involve murder – for example the PR thrillers by the former UK practitioner David Michie, the British PR man Graham Lancaster, or the US crisis management expert Eric Dezenhall – underlining just how much is at stake.

These fictional portrayals overlap with the depiction of real-life PR and PR people. It is worth analyzing this in some detail in order to try and identify the attractions of PR.

- *Notwithstanding its anonymity, PR benefits from its high-profile and novelty value.*

   Although PR practitioners have been around since the early twentieth century in the United States, in most countries PR is a relative newcomer. Even in the United Kingdom, home of the largest

PR industry outside the United States, it only really emerged from its embryo in the 1980s. Nowadays there may be countless references to PR and PR stunts, but in many societies the novelty value lingers and attracts attention and interest as a result. The term "spin" has also become ubiquitous in recent years, further promoting interest in the field. To novelty value may be added curiosity value. For the reasons described above people know surprisingly little about the PR industry. PR has a certain mystique.

- *"Let's get celebritied up!"*[15]
  One of the principal attractions of PR is glamour – a perception that it brings PR practitioners into close proximity with the media and celebrities, both seen as glamorous in their own right. As an applicant for a PR course told one of the authors, her interest arose when she realized she could not be a celebrity herself: working in PR was the next best thing. Whatever else may be said about them, popular representations of PR such as *Sex and the City, Absolutely Fabulous* or Gwyneth Paltrow's PR woman in *Sliding Doors*, exude glamour. They portray PR people – usually women – leading exciting lives. They consort with the wealthy and famous, and their work is portrayed as one long party. Indeed, as mentioned earlier, some American viewers of *AbFab* believed the program represented a "manifesto for life." Edina, the anti-heroine of *AbFab*, whose character was in fact inspired by a real-life London PR woman, Lynne Franks,[16] displayed this through her fondness for celebrities, luxury goods, and travel. Part of the attraction is perhaps that some of the glamour and success will rub off on people joining the PR industry. In Daisy Waugh's novel *The New You Survival Kit* the London PR heroine is "Highly employable, admirably well-informed. Articulate. Intelligent. Financially autonomous."[17] The agency for which she works employs "Thirty-seven slim women and two fat ones (both secretaries), one West Indian post boy and three lean and well-dressed white men."[18]

- *PR is closely associated with whatever is newest, freshest, and most fashionable – and often most successful.*
  Its role in promoting new products and repositioning old ones helps PR to be seen as cutting-edge and contemporary. Unsurprisingly, whatever is currently in the news or in vogue is often closely associated with PR: PR and fashion – in its broadest sense – are inseparable. In one episode *Sex and the City's* Samantha Jones, who "never missed a major fashion show," handles the opening of the "hottest new restaurant in Manhattan." As she

turns away people at the door she mentions that some are actually crying. The restaurant has the hottest chef in New York: "Did I mention I'm sleeping with him?"[19]

- *PR also adores novelty for itself.*
  It is hard for PR people and PR consultancies to differentiate themselves and seek competitive advantage (ultimately the difference is about personalities, but this is notoriously hard to articulate convincingly). To get round this problem PR people are keen to show themselves keeping abreast of new technologies, new media, and new social developments. Although hard to quantify, this aura of modernity is attractive and something PR plays to.

- *PR epitomizes self-assured modern womanhood.*
  One thing many portrayals of "PR girls" have in common is that they have well-paid, interesting jobs, or indeed their own businesses. Indeed, although Gwyneth Paltrow's PR character is fired from her largely male PR company at the beginning of *Sliding Doors*, she is able to establish her own successful consultancy, and it is no coincidence that *AbFab*'s Edina Monsoon and *Sex and the City*'s Samantha Jones both run their own PR businesses. This theme is explored further in the next chapter.

- *Superficial, but rarely dull.*
  PR work might be stigmatized as superficial but is seldom portrayed as boring, unlike many alternative careers. It is a creative industry, with all the positive resonances that that has, rather than a respectable but predictable profession (see Chapter 8). In popular culture PR is often portrayed as a matter of thinking up ideas for events and parties and then attending them. This has a long history. In one of the first film portrayals of PR, the Oscar-winning *Waikiki Wedding* of 1937, Bing Crosby's PR man lolls around on a boat off Hawaii, contributing the occasional idea for publicity, while workers at the pineapple cannery that employs him get on with the drudgery of tinning fruit. *Sliding Doors* and *Sex and the City* display a party-filled existence. Even the most grudging PR people have to admit that PR work can involve lunches, receptions and parties which include meeting many different people in a range of locations. This is readily exaggerated for the small or large screen. Ordinary office work has always been difficult to portray on stage, screen, or on the page, since so much of what people do seems tedious. PR seems to be one of the exceptions. Indeed it may be that

one of the reasons PR is favored by film and TV producers is that it offers a perfect way of showcasing working life in modern cities. It is noteworthy, for example, that the character of Samantha Jones in the original novel *Sex and the City* was a film producer. Perhaps PR, the occupation chosen for the TV series, was thought better suited to a display of hedonistic nymphomania!

- *At the heart of things.*
The spin doctors mentioned earlier are shown dealing with the most important people in the organizations they serve and tackling the most pressing issues. After all, senior people in all organizations pay close personal attention to the media coverage they receive, and so PR people are to the fore. Errol Flynn, playing the first designated PR consultant to appear in a Hollywood film, says, "The heads of 120 corporations seek my advice,"[20] while Gregory Peck, playing an in-house practitioner in *The Man in a Grey Flannel Suit*, an adaptation of the 1950s bestselling novel, observes, "I've landed in one of the neatest positions in the whole organization, right next to Hopkins [the chief executive] himself. It's a spot that three-quarters of the people at UBC would give their right arms for."

The power of political and corporate PR men (and on occasion women) is hard to pin down, as so much of it depends on their relationship with the people for whom they work. But this in itself creates its own mystique. PR people at the pinnacle of the consultancy sector, where they work for a range of powerful clients, can claim, or be credited with, immense power, and can appear like spiders at the center of a carefully spun web. The male publicist in the movie *Phone Booth* is shown as powerful but also unscrupulous and manipulative. Similarly, the PR advocate for smoking in the novel and movie *Thank You for Smoking* is shown operating close to the seat of commercial power. He may be charming, but is hardly very moral. From the American movie *Primary Colors* to the BBC radio and TV series *Absolute Power* the stereotype is reiterated.

This cultural portrayal is reflected in the news media. Characters such as Lord Tim Bell, often seen as the PR man who made Margaret Thatcher acceptable to the British public, through to George W Bush's advisor, Karl Rove, and UK Prime Minister Tony Blair's advisor Alastair Campbell, were and are often referred to by the media as "spin doctors," "PR gurus," or "the PR power behind the throne." Their activities, which take place behind closed doors, exude a similar air of mystery. They are often just behind the headlines. (Lord Bell, who runs Britain's largest consultancy group, has more recently attracted attention for the advice he has given to two billionaires from the former Soviet Union, the late Badri Patarkatsishvili and Boris Berezovsky.) They may not always be liked, but they are generally respected and in some instances feared. Some people are attracted by this idea of wielding manipulative power.

The opening words of the PR patriarch Edward Bernays' book *Propaganda* are calculated to be memorable:

The conscious and intelligent manipulation of the organized habits and opinions of the masses is an important element in democratic society. Those who manipulate this unseen mechanism of society constitute an invisible government which is the true ruling power of our country.[21]

- *A quintessentially metropolitan lifestyle.*
  The lifestyle associated with PR is something many people find attractive. As an applicant for a PR course told one of the authors, she wanted to work in PR because it was "a city job." Spin doctors operate in corporate headquarters, financial centers and seats of government. "PR girls" are portrayed as all but synonymous with city living, and big cities – particularly London and New York – are usually the principal setting for representations of PR in popular culture. Indeed such fictional treatments become loving homages to life in those cities and the opportunities they offer.

- *Ease of entry.*
  Irwin Ross writing nearly fifty years ago observed how easy it was to start a PR consultancy. He described it as "one of the last frontiers open to free, exuberant and often quite impecunious private enterprise…Some practitioners make it in a few short years. A lot more try."[22]

  Employment in PR is not only expanding rapidly, but neither long apprenticeships nor specific qualifications are required. This is in marked contrast to established professions, which typically insist on degrees – and postgraduate degrees – in specific subjects, coupled with on-the-job training backed up with further exams.

PR people may opt to study public relations and undertake further training, but there is no requirement to do so. The hero of the 1950s film, *The Man in the Gray in the Gray Flannel Suit*, worried that he knows nothing about PR, is told by his friend: "Who does? You've got a clean shirt, you bathe every day, that's all there is to it."

This continues to contain a grain of truth. Although PR people often protest that their work should be seen as a proper profession, the fact that people can enter PR without committing themselves to prolonged, arduous training is undoubtedly an attraction.

- *Money.*
  Despite the lack of need for long apprenticeships, PR offers – and is certainly portrayed as offering – the prospect of earning a great deal of money. PR lifestyles are almost invariably displayed as opulent. This is backed up by the general sense that PR is a booming industry and that PR people are in demand, the subtext of most portrayals. While further research would be needed to confirm this, there is plenty of anecdotal evidence that this contributes to the appeal of PR in many emerging democracies and market economies, where the rise of PR is associated with progress, western ideas, economic growth, freedom, and democracy.

- *The variety of the work is appealing.*
  Although many celluloid depictions of PR focus on media relations, such as Bridget Jones' "fannying about with press releases," other aspects of PR work often surface, especially event management. PR people can work for almost any kind of organization. PR seems to offer would-be practitioners the opportunity to decide what interests them, do the PR for it, and get paid into the bargain. This is reflected in student interest in fashion, sports, music, and entertainment PR, even if the supply of jobs in these sectors may not match demand.[23] The universal applicability of PR techniques enables people to follow their interest almost anywhere – into politics and government, all areas of commerce and finance, and into charitable work and campaigning. PR seems to offer a dream – working in the music industry although you are not musical, or alongside footballers despite an inability to kick a ball.

Variety of work is also a function of the structure of the PR industry. Most PR people work in-house, within a wide variety of organizations, but a large minority work for PR consultancies that sell their services to a variety of clients, and there are plenty of freelance PR people. Many people's PR careers are a pick and mix of work in these different parts of the industry. PR consultancies can themselves be large or small, can specialize in offering particular PR services or serving particular sectors, or can offer a broad range of services to different clients. Consultancies are also simple to set up: plenty of successful ventures comprised little more than the right people and a little office equipment at the outset, and many people find this prospect enticing. As Samantha Jones puts it in Episode 1 of *Sex and the City*, distinguishing herself from the other three principal characters, "Hey, I'm as good looking as a model and I own my own business."

As she contemplates setting up her own consultancy Gwyneth Paltrow's character is told in *Sliding Doors*, "Do you want to spend the rest of your life working for other people?"

### A day in the life of a US PR professional

*Jenny Cain, Public Relations Manager, Belron United States, owners of Safelite AutoGlass.*

Working in the public relations profession means there is never a dull moment. Things are constantly changing everyday. So taking a snapshot of today's "day in the life," would most likely be different than tomorrow's "to do" list. There's always a plan of what you want to do, but often things will sidetrack your planned activities.

Each day starts off the same and ends the same ... listening to the news.

What's happened in the world since you went to sleep last night? Your ears tune in for news stories that might impact your business ... how could it influence your PR efforts? While you do that you key in your password to your Blackberry, which is never turned off, to see if there are any pertinent emails that might impact the morning schedule.

You arrive in the office and notice the news release that was drafted the day before is sitting on your chair with some edits from your boss. Your goal is to make those edits, identify the key media outlets it should go to and then get it out the door by end of business that day.

You dock your laptop and hit the power to start it up so you can review all the online news alerts that have come in to your email box since you left the day before and compile the daily industry news report that goes out to the key leadership of the company. Today's schedule includes a media interview with the company's CEO and a "prep" session in advance of the interview to go through potential questions that might be asked.

You dial your voice mail and find you have a message from a business reporter who saw a real estate transaction notice and wants to find out more about a new facility you are leasing in Spokane, Washington. You know nothing about it, so you make a note in your planner to call the real estate department and find out more. Later, you will add the contact information to the media contact report and return the call.

But first, you make copies of the two pages of talking points drafted for the CEO for his media interview and head off to the prep session in his office. Everything goes as planned and you let the CEO know you'll greet the reporter at the appointed time and bring him to his office for the interview.

During the interview, you take meticulous notes in case anything needs to be clarified later. The reporter has a few numbers-related questions that you must research and get back to him about later.

Back at your desk you receive a call from a field manager saying a TV station has contacted him to do an on-camera interview about work being done by the company in his market. You assess the purpose of the interview and segment and advise the manager that it's OK to proceed. You tell the manager you will watch for the clip and send out copies of it to him.

You call to confirm the arrangements made last week with a newspaper photographer who is scheduled to shoot photos of the CEO in the morning to accompany the article from today's interview. You advise the CEO that everything is set and that you will meet him at the facility in the morning. He asks, so you give advice on which tie would work best for the photo shoot.

Back at your desk you begin to wrap up the day's events. You check news alerts and then head out the door. You turn on the radio in your car and listen to the news. It's come full circle … you are thinking about what you are hearing and how it might impact your business … how could it influence our PR efforts?

To understand PR's attractions properly they have to be put into context, as students and would-be PR people do not consider their careers in a vacuum but alongside possible alternatives. Established professions not only require considerable commitment and long periods of training, but can also seem dull and stuffy. Within its own media and marketing services sector PR has growing attractions. Compared with journalism the prospects are better: it now offers more jobs at higher salaries and with better working conditions. In the United States and United Kingdom public relations has overtaken advertising as a source of employment,[24] and is rightly regarded as offering more varied career opportunities. Compared with marketing, which is sometimes perceived as a somewhat dry discipline, PR is often seen as offering more human interest and more scope for intuition: PR remains an art not a science and thus appeals to the creative.

PR is perhaps the ultimate postmodern industry. No one knows what it really is, but it sounds interesting!

# Girls, gurus, gays, and diversity

## PR's strange social profile

Not to be crass, but is PR viewed as a "chick" degree?[1]

Public Relations is an overwhelmingly female occupation and yet its summit is still predominantly peopled by males. Why is this? Does it matter? What – if indeed anything needs doing – can be done about it?

The numbers are revealing. In the United States it is estimated that 65% of practitioners are women, while the latest figures from the Public Relations Society of America point to 90% female membership.[2] In the UK's Chartered Institute of Public Relations (CIPR – until recently just the IPR) figures estimate 62% of practitioners are female.[3] Meanwhile in France it is estimated that 80% of all PR practitioners are women.[4]

### Girls

But it seems PR is not only a predominantly female occupation now but is getting more so by the year. At entry level, those who want to enter PR are overwhelmingly female.[5] At the University of Westminster in London the intake on postgraduate PR courses is over 90% female. On the undergraduate courses it is only a little lower at around 80%. The numbers at Kent State University in America are similar.[6] When the authors lecture to PR students at the Sorbonne in Paris the picture is more or less the same.

What can be driving this extraordinary influx of women into an industry which, as we shall see later, still appears to deny them the top jobs? One driver is undoubtedly popular culture. As we saw in Chapter 1 PR is portrayed on the big and small screen as a sexy, fast moving, well-paid and exciting job that is welcoming to women.

But, however popular many of these portrayals are, they are also often sexist. The image of superficial and frivolous fun lovers is encapsulated in the term "PR girls."

Most people with direct experience of the PR industry have experienced slighting references to "PR girls" – even hearing them from their female colleagues. The stereotype is captured in a book title, *Big Smiles in Short Skirts Won't Work!: Corporate Communications for Professional Service Companies.*[7] Or as Bridget Jones's boss puts it, "You swan in in your short skirt and your sexy see-through blouse."

But despite the pejorative tone of some of the popular depictions of women in PR, female applicants are not put off. Far from it.

## Gurus

The portrayals of women in PR are in contrast to the depictions of men, which are much darker yet display them wielding more power. PR men at the very top of the industry are often referred to as "PR gurus". Senior PR women are seldom described in this way. Nor, for different reasons, are lawyers, accountants, or doctors. Taken out of its original religious context – as it now normally is – the term "Guru" is generally used to describe either the leader of a cult or someone who is perceived as an expert in area that lacks conventional frames of reference for measuring expertise, such as those found in the sciences and conventional professions. Hence "fashion guru," "style guru," and "PR guru."

So given the powerful portrayal of men and the rather "fluffy" portrayal of women in PR, why is it that there are so many women and, relatively speaking, so few men? And why do men still seem to hold more senior positions and, in general, earn more?

In 2008, *PR Week* in the UK produced a "Power Book."[8] It described itself as "the definitive guide to the most influential people in PR." Sixty-nine percent of the entrants were men and just thirty-one percent women – more or less the reverse of the current gender split in the industry.

Not surprisingly the reasons for this are similar to those for the fact that men with five or more years experience in PR still, on average, earn more than their female counterparts ($124,000 median salary for men versus $85,000 for women according to a 2007 survey).[9] There is no evidence that women are paid less for directly comparable jobs (in many countries including the United Kingdom and United States this would be illegal). The differences are based on age, experience, and industry sector.

Men are on average older and have been in PR longer, with an average age of 38 and average industry experience of 11.1 years against an average female age of 33.8 and experience of 8.2 years.[10] (These age and experience figures are undoubtedly high and reflect the weakness of surveys. Respondents are a self-selecting group. In our view older practitioners are more likely to respond.) Inevitably increased pay goes hand in hand with age and experience. As more women enter the profession and accumulate experience the differential should reduce.

Another factor is likely to be that, according to a survey by UK-based Women in PR conducted in 2002,[11] fewer than half of the women in PR who were married or co-habiting were the main bread winners. Again, while it is impossible to prove, this fact may lessen the motivation of some women to maximize their earnings at the possible cost of their job satisfaction. Moreover women still tend to be the key child carers and take career breaks or even give up their career as they start to have children. Whatever the rights and wrongs of these patterns, they may affect the make-up of the industry.

Men are also far better represented in the higher earning sectors, such as lobbying and financial PR. According to the same survey of female PRs by Women in PR, 70% of respondents worked in consumer and lifestyle PR, traditionally less remunerative than financial PR and lobbying and public affairs. There is insufficient space here to explore why men are better represented in financial and political PR, but suffice it to say that politics and finance remain realms dominated by men. It would not be surprising if these sectors both attracted and showed a preference – possibly subconscious – for male PRs.

It is noteworthy that at the junior levels of lower account executive/PR officer the pay differential is virtually non-existent. Time will show if this is because the factors described above are not significant at an early stage in people's careers, or if it represents a real change.

There is no public evidence that a majority of women in the industry believe there is glass ceiling holding them back or that they are discriminated against. According to the Women in PR survey over half are "satisfied" or "very satisfied" that women in PR were not discriminated against, with only a quarter thinking there might be some discrimination. However, a quarter felt under pressure from family life and the sound of eager young entrants knocking at the door.

## Why are there more women in PR?

According to Women in PR there are seven main reasons why there are so many women in the industry:

1. They are better, or natural, communicators (33%);
2. They multitask and organize better than men (23%);
3. PR is a soft career suited to women – as are teaching, human resources etc. (18%);
4. They have better and more sensitive "people skills" (18%);
5. They are better able to pay attention to detail and to look at things from different perspectives (15%);
6. They are better suited to a variety of practical administrative tasks (10%); and
7. Women have greater imagination, intuition, and are sensitive to nuances (8%).

As we will explain, we think PR is about persuading people to think or behave in a particular way. The ability to persuade has two elements. The first is the ability to reason – to marshal and deploy the available evidence in a way likely to secure the desired outcome. The second is empathy – the ability to understand the audience being targeted and to present the evidence for your case in the way that is most likely to be emotionally persuasive. Great PR is about winning hearts as well as minds.

Setting aside what the reaction would be to a survey of men, and by men, that claimed men were more logical than women, arguing that women have more empathy than men seems reasonable and is supported by a number of serious studies including one from the Autism Research Centre at the University of Cambridge.[12] It is also the common currency of populist works such as *Men are from Mars, Women are from Venus*.[13]

Two other reasons are sometimes given for the preponderance of women in PR. One is that the industry is particularly child friendly. We can find no real evidence for this in comparison to other forms of employment. Although PR can lend itself to freelance activity and working from home, much of the PR industry, particularly on the consultancy side, is characterized by long hours, late nights, and hard work. Furthermore, with most major PR consultancies being based in crowded city centers there is often little access to local childcare facilities. Some of the main reasons given for the high churn rate in PR, particularly at the middle level, are to do with long hours, relatively low pay, and lack of job satisfaction.[14]

The other argument, generally put forward by women, is that women are suited to the background role often adopted by the PR practitioner: "Their professional brief decrees that PR women pull strings and work hard – but remain content to sit back and bask in reflected glory."[15] Or, as a female PR practitioner says, "Maybe that self-effacement is one reason women are good at PR. PR is often played out in the background. The executive is the star, the PR person is invisible."[16] This seems to be a simple extension of the empathy point. However, a word of caution is needed. Other "background" activities such as accountancy are far more male in their makeup.

Does the feminization of PR matter? The current evidence would seem to be that it does not. The industry by almost any measure continues to grow and outperform the wider economy. PR courses in universities and colleges are often oversubscribed and show no signs of decreasing in number. What is there not to like?

There are other sectors dominated by one sex that continue to thrive. Human resources, large parts of retail, teaching, and nursing are dominated by women. Wall Street and the City, the engineering and the petroleum and chemical industries are dominated by men. The only problems these gender disparities seem to cause are ones of image. They run counter to the accepted orthodoxy that there should be equality of the sexes.

But should not a modern business discipline, particularly one concerned with people and communication, accurately reflect the composition of society? This sounds reasonable. So would PR be a better, more effective, more respected industry if it employed more men? The answer to this may lie in the fact that it used to employ a much larger proportion of men and was at that time a much smaller, and no more or less respected, industry.

The flexible nature of entry to the industry means that the number of men could be swiftly increased if there was a business case for it. Moreover in certain specialist fields of public relations such as financial PR and lobbying there is a shortage of women rather than men. Overall there seem to be no more complaints about gender disparities than in other industries.

**Day in the Life Marlin W. Collingwood Managing Director Bell Pottinger USA**

| | |
|---|---|
| 6:30 a.m. | Review and respond to overnight emails from London offices. |
| 6:45 a.m. | Check office voice mail for any overnight messages from London offices. |
| 7:00 a.m. | Read *New York Times* and *Boston Globe* at home. |
| 7:30 a.m. | Leave for office. |
| | Return two calls to London via Blackberry while driving to office. |
| 8:00 a.m. | Arrive at office. |
| | Scan online newspapers for client news including *Pittsburgh Post-Gazette*, *Chicago Tribune*, *Wall Street Journal* and *Philadelphia Inquirer*. |
| 8:30 a.m. | Return overnight phone calls and emails from London. |
| 9:30 a.m. | Staff meeting with senior staff with client and media updates. |
| 10:30 a.m. | Conference call with client attorneys regarding ongoing acquisition plans and possible press announcement regarding plans. |
| 11:15 a.m. | Conference call with sister agency in London regarding mutual client and upcoming US trade show plans. |
| 12:30 p.m. | Lunch outside of office with Boston Globe energy reporter regarding one of our renewable fuels clients and an upcoming announcement. |
| 2:00 p.m. | Final rehearsal of new business presentation set for later in the week. |
| 3:30 p.m. | Briefing call with client and New York Times reporter who is planning a Sunday feature story on client CEO. |
| 4:00 p.m. | Weekly call with health insurance client communications team addressing issues upcoming for the week, possible media inquiries, and any potential crisis situations. |
| 5:00 p.m. | Video conference with California-based client to review legislative hearing testimony for upcoming US Senate Appropriations Committee hearing where client CEO is testifying. |
| 6:00 p.m. | Depart for airport for trip to New York City. |
| 8:00 p.m. | Dinner in New York City with client and Wall Street Journal reporter regarding product launch. |
| 10:00 p.m. | Final review of talking points and press release for client product announcement set for tomorrow morning @ 9:30 a.m. |

## Gays

The importance of empathy may also explain another characteristic of PR: the high proportion of gay men. Informed estimates of the proportion of homosexuals within the population vary, but seem to converge around the 3 to 6% mark.[17] If PR reflected society this would suggest that around one in twenty men working in the industry would be gay. However observation and anecdotal evidence from our student intake and PR consultancies – particularly in the consumer and lifestyle fields, but also in lobbying – suggests the figure is far higher, certainly for male homosexuals (representation of lesbians appears to be much less pronounced).

We have been unable to find any figures estimating th proportion of male homosexuals working in public relations. This might indicate either that it is a taboo question that researchers feel unable to ask, or that it is not seen as an issue worthy of investigation. We suspect the former. After all, we are apprehensive about mentioning this subject despite it being a commonplace observation in the PR world. Gender and ethnicity are accepted research categories. There is little danger of suffering prejudice as a result of *stating* obvious characteristics, such as your sex and ethnicity. But sexual preference is not immediately apparent, and until recently homophobic prejudice has been legal and all too common. Disclosure could be used against the respondent; the matter is deemed private rather than an accepted research category.

Whether gay men, on average, have more empathy than heterosexual men is a question beyond the scope of this book. We would welcome the thoughts of gay, lesbian, and straight people within the industry. There may be other parallels between the employment of gay men and women. Once the industry has shown itself to be welcoming to a few women or indeed gay men others quickly follow. There is also the possibility that the dominance of women and the relatively large numbers of gay men may make some straight men decide that the industry is not for them. We have been told by students from some developing nations that there is a perception in their country that only gay men work in PR. Lingering prejudices may act as a disincentive to men joining the PR industry in such countries.[18]

## Ethnic mix

If we can afford to be fairly relaxed about the high proportion of women in PR, can we be equally relaxed about the low percentage of people from nonwhite backgrounds?

There is no doubt that the PR industry does not offer a proper reflection of society's ethnic and racial mix, although things are improving. According to a CIPR survey in 2005, 6.5% of UK PRs were from ethnic minority groups compared with 8% of the UK population.[19] Similarly 89.4% of the US PR industry is white compared to 82.2% of the whole population.[20] More important than these overall figures is, however, our suspicion that some of the least privileged ethnic minority communities are barely represented at all.

In both the United Kingdom and the United States a few firms run by people from ethnic minorities specialize in reaching minority audiences. Do these firms compound and maintain differences that might otherwise wither? And if, as some argue, only people from ethnic minorities can effectively understand and reach minorities, does that mean that those same ethnic minority PR practitioners are unable effectively to understand and reach the white majority?

It would seem to be commonsense that the industry should try to reflect the composition of the society that it serves, though the fact that it does not has hardly limited its growth. Unequal demographic representation would appear to be more a problem of image than substance – and yet the PR industry is in large part about the management of image.

> I think a bit more diversity in terms of race and social background would be healthy for an industry now at the heart of consumer, media, and social change.
>
> Colin Byrne, CEO, UK and Ireland Shandwick PR[21]

# CHAPTER 3

# PR and the media
## A love/hate relationship

**Why are there more flacks than hacks?**

> The day I can't get along without a press agent's handouts, I'll close up shop and move to Alaska, lock, stock and barrel.[1]

The Public Relations industry in part owes its origins a century ago to the need US corporations felt to defend themselves against the increasingly strident mass media of the day, the muckrakers of the Yellow Press, the mass circulation newspapers of the United States. At the time big business was inarticulate and on the defensive, good at making money but seldom effective at engaging with public opinion.[2]

Times have changed. The mass media may seem more dominant than ever, but while numbers of journalists have grown the increase has not kept up with the exponential growth in media production. Not only do we now expect media organizations to provide broadcast coverage around the clock from an infinite number of channels, but we expect bigger newspapers with more pages and more supplements, and more and fatter magazines. We also expect the same news organizations to maintain extensive websites.

Media organizations are under increasing pressure. In many countries advertising revenue is migrating away from traditional media while the fragmentation of advertising-funded broadcasting means that many more channels have to be paid for out of a similar-sized or shrinking pot. Costly public sector broadcasters such as the BBC face mounting difficulties as their right to raise funds through disguised taxation is increasingly challenged. Newspaper circulations in the developed world are dwindling, while the search for a successful payment model for online news media continues. This pressure on income has led to a struggle to control costs. Specialist journalists with many years of experience lose out to less-experienced but cheaper general reporters. Subeditors become an costly luxury. Sending journalists out to investigate stories is expensive, offering no certainty of a return on expenditure. But keeping journalists in the office, tied to their computers, makes it much easier to assess their productivity.

For his 2008 book, *Flat Earth News*, the UK journalist Nick Davies commissioned research from Cardiff University about the sources of UK news stories in Britain's five most prestigious national newspapers.[3]

The research found that 60% of the stories comprised wholly or mainly PR material and/or wire (news agency) copy, and a further 20% contained clear elements of wire copy and/or PR. Forty-one percent of wire copy contained clear signs of PR. Overall PR material found its way into 54% of the stories. In 8% of cases the source was unclear. In only 12% of cases was the material generated by the reporters themselves.

Davies also found that average staffing levels were slightly lower than twenty years before, but the amounts of editorial space had trebled.[4]

Although this valuable research confirms the dominant role of PR, it probably understates the position.

- Davies and his researchers focused on a handful of well-known national newspapers which still employ large numbers of journalists. Less successful media outlets are by definition even more dependent on the "free" content which PR can supply. Davies acknowledges this and his own accounts of the pressures on provincial journalists confirm it.
- Davies' research focuses on UK news stories. These represent newspapers' traditional core business, and are likely to be relatively well served by reporting staff. The proportion of

PR content is likely to be much higher in the newer and rapidly expanding sections of the newspaper press which cover topics such as celebrities, fashion, travel, property, culture, personal finance, and motoring.

- It is likely that a proportion of the 12% of stories allegedly generated by journalists were in fact indirectly triggered by PR – without the journalist necessarily being aware of it. In practice journalists seldom chance upon stories. They are normally prompted in some way. Even if the prompt comes from a friend, colleague or contact, or from elsewhere in the media, it is more than likely to have been sparked by PR in some guise. The best PR, after all, is invisible.

Nor is this simply a UK phenomenon. A *Columbia Journalism Review* study found that over half the stories in an edition of the *Wall Street Journal* "were based solely on press releases," reprinted "almost verbatim or in paraphrase."[5]

Meanwhile PR has grown from its negligible beginnings in the early twentieth century into a large and still-swelling industry. In the United States, the most advanced economy, there are more PR people than journalists, and this is now true in the United Kingdom.[6] In Britain, well within the memories of many current PR people, large organizations often did not feel the need to maintain a PR function. Now in-house PR departments are ubiquitous, and are supplemented by a large consultancy sector. Many countries are heading in the same direction. But because this is a relatively recent phenomenon, and one that is still taking shape in many societies, it has not received the attention it deserves. Scholarship operates with a time lag, and remains more comfortable with studying the declining newspaper industries of the developed world than the newer world of PR. Nor has the relationship of mutual dependence between PR and journalism, one that is so fundamental to the modern media, been much examined. Even at a scholarly level the relationship between PR and the media continues to be the empty quarter of the study of mass communication, occasionally commented on but little researched (see Chapter 11).[7]

Put simply, what has happened is that modern organizations, be they governmental, commercial, charitable, or otherwise, find it worthwhile to spend an increasing share of their resources on managing the media. In many societies PR people are now more highly paid and enjoy better working conditions and better career prospects than their counterparts in journalism. The resources at their command are often greater too. Journalism by contrast is increasingly denuded of resources as well as staff, whittling away at its ability to generate its own news content and to cross-check what it is being told. All of this means that the balance of power has shifted, and continues to shift, in favor of PR.

PR also benefits from its clarity of purpose. It is – despite a few noises-off from would-be industry moralists – about persuading people to act in particular ways in the interests of the people who pay for it. How it goes about this may be the subject of debate, but the objective is clear. Journalism's search for a purpose is much more fraught and agonizing. What is often portrayed as a crusade for truth is trapped within the commercial imperatives of business: journalists talk about objectivity and the importance of investigation, but have to work within the constraints of mounting anxiety about circulation and ratings, sales and advertising. The tension may be creative but it also creates problems. Many journalists recoil from the notion that they work in an entertainment industry, yet to a considerable extent they do, and this is an arena where PR people can help them.

Journalists not infrequently pass comments on PR. The remarks below by well-known British journalists repay a little examination.

Bryan Appleyard: "Hacks, at least the ones I'd have round to dinner, still naively pursue something they like to call the truth. Their problem is that it no longer exists. For truth has been destroyed by public relations executives or 'scum' as we like to call them. Power has shifted from the editors to the PRs."[8]

Rod Liddle: "We don't have much to cling on to as journalists. I try to think that it's a noble trade. Pretty much the only thing we have is our independence and distance from the people who wish to make money or gain power. PR people are in a parasitical occupation."[9]

Liddle, formerly the editor of what is perhaps the UK's top talk radio show, the *Today Programme* on BBC Radio 4, talks up journalistic ideals, in his case emphasizing independence. However his words are tinged with a note of defeat: he can only *try* to think journalism is a noble trade. Like his fellow-journalists he makes himself feel better by having a swing at PR. Similarly Bryan Appleyard, also a columnist at *The Sunday Times*, neatly sums up journalistic ideals and a not uncommon embittered journalistic attitude to PR people. Sadly, there seems little attempt to come to terms with the world as it is rather than as they wish it was.

An enormous amount of what appears in the media originates in the hands of PR people. PR's impact on what we read, see, and hear spills over from news and current affairs into entertainment and drama. The media's modes of production and, very importantly, their costs of production, assume the existence of a well-resourced PR industry able to supply or, at the very least help with, the production of media content.

This dependency seldom breaks surface, but when it does journalists and their editors have the last word. They may deplore spin and praise transparency, but are seldom prepared to reveal all about how they come by their stories, although an honest list of the ingredients of most news stories, and the recipes according to which they were prepared, would be an eye-opener. This reluctance is only in small part about protecting sources. It has much more to do with the unwillingness of magicians to reveal how they perform their tricks, and reflects an understandable unwillingness to admit how much of the fare the media supply to their customers is delivered "oven-ready" by the PR industry. Confessing to the truth would undermine the self-image of journalists as fearless seekers after the truth, as ideals of independence and objectivity are hard to reconcile with dependence on PR people.

On the other side of the fence PR people may not be wholly reliable witnesses, as they oscillate between a desire for self-promotion and the need to keep mum. Some may boastfully overstate their influence and their ability to exert control over the media. Others seek to draw a veil over their achievements for a reason. After all, the aim of gaining positive media coverage is to make readers, viewers, and listeners think that what they are seeing or hearing is not just a paid-for advertisement, but the outcome of a journalist's independent work. PR effectiveness is closely associated with not being noticed.

If journalists and PR people are unreliable witnesses with their own axes to grind, independent investigation of the impact of PR on the media faces its own problems – surely the reason scholars so often duck the issue. Researchers who are accustomed to using archives find that the most interesting and controversial aspects of PR typically leave a scant and unreliable paper trail. Much of the real meat of PR lies in conversations and private meetings, among PR people and between PR people and journalists. The conversations take place between protagonists who often know each other well, and who understand the stakes at play; much is left unsaid or only hinted at or implied. Such words as are used are seldom fully or reliably reported, although occasionally, as we see elsewhere in this book, light is shed on the more sensational aspects of PR when conversations are secretly recorded or unguarded emails are leaked.

Line by line analyses of media reports are potentially rewarding. Often – as we shall see – journalists may be unconscious that they are using recycled PR, or may salve their consciences by relying on a variety of PR sources, turning to different or opposed organizations for comment in order to introduce balance to their reports. This may be a respectable practice but still represents dependence on PR: at one level the journalist can amount to little more than an observer in a game of ping pong, summarizing the different, opposed views of the protagonists in the story.

For even the most conscientious journalist it can be hard to know exactly when they are dealing with PR: it does not come clearly labeled. One instance of this, which we look at in more detail later, is the way journalists cover the activities of charities and campaigning organizations without focusing on the fact that the activities are in themselves public relations and that such bodies are large-scale users of PR, even if they would seldom use the term to describe what they do. Journalists also deal with many other people performing a PR role without necessarily being identifiable as "PR practitioners": the role of political leaders, for example, has always overlapped with PR since the work of any politician has a media relations dimension.

Books on the subject sometimes hazard suspiciously rounded percentages for the proportion of newsprint originating in PR. The figures vary enormously: estimates of the proportion of what is sometimes termed "placed news" range up to 80%.[10] But another way of approaching the subject is to pose a different question: if journalists do not get their stories from PR then where else do they obtain them? Clearly a journalist may witness a newsworthy event, but for increasingly desk-bound journalists this is even less likely than a police officer on patrol happening upon a crime. Sometimes an individual with a story may approach a news organization directly, although more and more often they seek PR advice first. Again, some journalists frequent venues which are deemed likely to generate news – legislatures, law courts (in the most famous drama about journalism, *The Front Page*, the journalists are of course clustered in a press room close to a condemned man's cell) – but the forces of PR are often in attendance and usually have their input there as well. Moreover the economic straightjacket which constrains the media means journalists are less and less able to lie in wait for stories. In practice, if a journalist witnesses a newsworthy event it is usually because he or she has been alerted to it, and this can often be traced back to PR.

Much of what journalists write is gleaned from perusing other media, the offerings of news agencies, or information exchanged among media colleagues. Such material is no longer ostensibly PR-based – but again if one traces it back to its original source that is often what it is. A successfully managed piece of PR can snowball its way through the media, appearing in different news outlets and re-emerging in the comment and feature pages, gossip columns, and elsewhere. As the snowball grows the original press release, briefing, or tip-off will be lost to view. The PR practitioner may no longer need to intervene. Ideally – from a PR perspective, given the craving for third party endorsement – the media will feel it owns the story.

PR's role as a content supplier to the media has been termed "information subsidy."[11] There is no such thing as a free lunch, and the material supplied by PR people is prepared with a persuasive purpose in mind. The cumulative effect of this has led some to point to the PR-ization of the media,[12] raising the specter that the media will lose the reputation for independence and objectivity which made it such a valuable vehicle for PR people in the first place. This is particularly evident in those pages, supplements, and programs which cover not traditional "hard news" but fashion, food, property, leisure, sport, culture, travel, fashion, personal finance, and so on. It is hard to imagine the emergence of such media content without

PR (and related advertising), and it is here that PR has most palpably shaped the modern media.

There is little evidence, however, of public awareness of the extent of PR-related content in the media, and two important qualifications must be borne in mind. First, even if most news media content is PR-driven, most PR fails to feature in the news media. An oversupply of "news" from a well-resourced PR industry means that most press releases are simply discarded, calls to journalists are often not acted upon, and many press conferences are thinly attended. Critics of PR tend to focus on the machinations of the upper echelons of government and big corporations, but most PR activity is far more humble and much more readily ignored. Second, even if there is coverage, no PR person can ever be wholly certain of its nature and extent.

> "public relations people ... are better paid than all but handful of very senior or celebrity journalists; they also frequently have access to better technology and support systems. Some would say, but this is more controversial, that they are also better disciplined, more professional, and more skilful, and that this is the main reason journalism is in danger of being outsmarted."
>
> Ian Hargreaves, former Director of News and Current Affairs at the BBC and former Editor of *The Independent*.[13]

## Suppressing bad news: PR's dark side of the moon

> They should have had the power to keep it out of the papers ... that is half the job of a good PR.[14]

The even less-publicized side of media relations work, PR's dark side of the moon, is the role it plays in suppressing or at least minimizing the reporting of bad news. PR is commonly portrayed as being about the *promotion* of news stories: the attempt to get name checks or positive stories written about its paymasters. This is the usual focus of PR training and of PR textbooks, and when PR campaigns are described in trade publications this is what is usually featured. However PR plays an important part in exercising a mild form of censorship, although its practitioners would run away from the term. In the main informal pressures and inducements are used to try to suppress unwanted coverage. Indeed Aeron Davies, in his study of corporate PR, found that up to 50% of activity was devoted to lowering the profiles of organizations or blocking journalists.[15] The scale of this activity reflects the fact that, for the most part, journalists find bad news – stories about problems and arguments – more enticing than good news.

PR's censorship role starts within the organization. It is normal for organizations to insist on all relations with the media being channeled through their PR staff – and failure to comply with this can lead to disciplinary action or dismissal. The general notion that bringing one's employer into disrepute is a sackable offence helps strengthen the position of employers. Even when non-PR staff are allowed to speak to the media their employers usually impose strict controls on the nature of the exchanges and the type of information they are allowed to impart. Often such contacts are arranged and directly supervised by PR staff. Indeed establishing and maintaining tight control over an organization's relations with the media is fundamental to the success of PR work: any organization that does not speak with a single agreed voice will be picked apart. But PR people's informal powers to manage the media go well beyond exerting control over their own territory.

## The information marketplace: trading news and views

The promotion of good news and the playing down of bad news come together in what we term the *information marketplace*, the virtual forum where journalism and PR meet. Each side has to trade with the other, and each wants something out of the bargain. PR people have a range of techniques at their disposal, some means of leverage, and some ability to exploit their knowledge of the market. Indeed former journalists have tended to thrive in PR because of their knowledge of market conditions.

PR people have different degrees of power in the information marketplace depending on whom they represent. It is similar for journalists. Specialist journalists have more power: their accumulated knowledge and range of contacts enables them to be more discerning as they look for and prepare stories. Journalists working for media organizations which are prepared to invest in prolonged investigations also wield greater power. Finally, "big-name" journalists, typically people with major by-lines, have more bargaining power than junior reporters and often feel freer to express strong and controversial views. However the balance of power has shifted: while the PR industry has swollen and has ever greater resources at its disposal, the number of specialist journalists has dwindled, and investigative journalism has become an expensive luxury, often dreamed about but much more rarely practiced.

## News out of nothing

Perhaps 70% of PR jobs are marketing related and are about trying to sell goods and services.[16] Although companies naturally want to avoid critical coverage, the main problem in this section of the information marketplace is getting any kind of coverage at all. If all the new products being promoted were featured in the media we would see and hear about little else, and so it is in this part of the PR–media arena that one finds snowdrifts of unused press releases and can witness much of the desperate cold-calling by PR people about which journalists so often complain. Nonetheless some big or important companies and PR agencies will be able to exert leverage: a preview of an important new fashion collection or a new computer gadget is a valuable commodity, and being excluded from such possibilities could harm a journalist's standing.

> But the biggest question is whether advertising limits and reshapes the news agenda. It does, of course. It's hard to make the sums add up when you're kicking the people of who write the cheques.
>
> Andrew Marr, former Editor of *The Independent* [17]

The interplay with advertising is important. It is understood, to the point that it seldom needs saying, that, with rare exceptions such as the BBC, the media are dependent on advertising for most or all of their funding, and that that advertising comes from many of the same companies that are interested in promoting their messages through PR. Many of the newspaper supplements and magazines with specialized content are heavily reliant on advertising from their particular sectors. The pressure on editorial content, while usually remaining subtle and unstated, is twofold. In a broad sense the media is loathe to bite the hand that feeds it: property supplements do not attack the property industry; women's magazines do not attack the fashion industry and so on. By the same token an education supplement kept afloat by advertisements for teaching jobs is hardly going to launch a sustained attack on the quality of the teaching profession. Second, individual advertisers, if important enough, can wield specific power and ensure favorable editorial content for their products (or, alternatively, that unfavorable stories do not appear). These pressures are a taboo subject, and normally remain undocumented.

In 2004 a book, *Louis Vuitton: A French Saga*, was published in France. It alleged that the long-established and well-known French luxury luggage company had collaborated with the pro-Nazi Vichy regime after France's defeat at the hands of Germany in 1940. The book described how Louis Vuitton ran a factory which produced artifacts glorifying the regime's leader, Marshal Petain, and how it became the only company allowed to run a shop within the building used by the regime as its seat of government.

The Louis Vuitton Moet-Hennessy Group, the company's current owners, did not dispute the facts in the book. Despite this, these seemingly newsworthy revelations were hardly reported in the French media. Why? A newspaper article in the UK drew attention to the fact that Louis Vuitton is France's biggest advertiser. A company spokesperson told *Le Canard Enchaine*, a satirical magazine and the only French media outlet to report the story: "We haven't put any pressure on anyone. If the journalists want to censor themselves, then that suits us fine."[18]

However marketing PR also has to be creative and ingenious, creating irresistible stories and images that the media will want to use. To be successful, PR of this kind has to focus on what might be of interest to the media and, by extension, their readers, viewers, and listeners. Practitioners become adept users of what have been termed *pseudo-events*, events in which any action or content is essentially symbolic and which are organized to achieve publicity.[19] Indeed one way of looking at this aspect of the PR industry is as an industry which shadows the media it wishes to supply, studying its needs closely and deploying considerable resources, creativity, and bought-in journalistic skills to create its irresistible products. While newsworthiness is a slippery concept, successful PR people have an instinct for what makes a good story, an instinct which they nurture by studying the media. They are thus aware of what is right for different media outlets: a local angle for local media; a trade angle for specialist trade papers; strong visual material for television; or different angles and levels of coverage to suit the varying needs of national newspapers. While the resulting media coverage usually contains the desired namecheck for the organization concerned, it seldom makes it clear that the media's customers are receiving a PR product.

PR of this kind often includes the following, overlapping ingredients:

- Celebrity involvement
- Facts and figures from surveys
- Expert endorsement
- Publicity stunts and photo-opportunities
- Humor
- Human interest stories and case studies
- Competitions
- Sponsorship and charitable tie-ins

The British budget hotel chain Travelodge is a particularly adept user of proactive PR techniques. In autumn 2007 it featured regularly in the UK media, using a range of techniques drawn from those above. For example:

- It publicized the case of a couple who had chosen to live in a Travelodge hotel for 22 years.
- Its "annual sleepwalking audit" revealed a rise in the number of naked male sleepwalkers.
- It analyzed which cities in Britain had the biggest snoring problem (the worst example was Coventry!).
- It published a study showing the benefits to tourism of London hosting the 2012 Olympics.

- It announced the creation of a £25 million bounty payable to members of the public who help Travelodge find new sites for their hotels.
- The establishment of Britain's only professional Santa School at a central London hotel was topically announced in mid-November.
- It publicized plans to recruit more long-term unemployed as hotel staff.
- Announcing the opening of a new London hotel, Travelodge said it would feature the first "kipshaw" service – rickshaws fitted with single beds on which guests could snooze as they traveled to central London.
- Numerous hotel openings around the country, typically involving celebrities and prominent local people, were publicized.

But Travelodge did not stop there. They also invented new services such as the cuddle pillow for guests who were missing their partners, and a goldfish bowl hire service – apparently looking at goldfish helps you go to sleep.

As all this illustrates, Travelodge demonstrate keen news-sense. They managed to raid their own larder for newsworthy material, such as the story of their long-term guests. They also succeeded in publicizing research on a range of topics related to the hotel industry. Some were simply quirky and amusing and reported as such, some were more serious and worthy but potentially significant, such as the report on the benefits of the Olympics. Meanwhile industry-based stories and accounts of local hotel openings would appeal to the hospitality trade press and local media respectively.

Given Travelodge's rather prosaic business, their PR team managed to generate an impressive range of stories and secure an enormous number of name checks for the company, thereby demonstrating their awareness of the media's needs and likely interests.[20]

## Motivating the media: sticks and carrots

PR people working for more powerful organizations have a different relationship with the media. At best they can afford to treat journalists like obstinate and unreliable mules by applying a judicious mixture of sticks and carrots. They know the juiciest carrot a journalist can be offered is an important exclusive or "scoop." Journalists' careers and the reputations of the media organizations which they serve are made of such things – indeed a regular supply of the right kind of exclusives is worth far more than most bribes. Beyond the scoop itself, journalists depend on assistance from their PR contacts: without tip-offs, extra help with routine enquiries and so on, journalistic life becomes very difficult. It follows that the "stick" is to deny journalists exclusives and any general help or assistance. In some cases this can have fatal consequences for their career path, especially if the organization is dominant in the sector concerned.

> It is hard to document the use of the stick, but some years ago the aviation correspondent of a British national newspaper wrote articles that were critical of British Airways. BA took exception to this and made it clear to the journalist that he could expect no further help from them. Such is the importance of the national carrier that his career as an aviation correspondent was effectively over. He was last heard of working for a local radio station.[21]

### Standard techniques for managing news coverage

*New for old.* As mentioned above, what journalists prize above all is exciting news that is exclusive to them. PR people can present the same information in different forms. Since journalists are seldom specialists in the subjects which they report, if they can be convinced that the story is new they will often report it as such. Conversely, if it is possible to convince them that bad news is old news and has already been covered they often lose interest.

*Managing expectations.* What constitutes news is governed by journalists' expectations. Were a highly successful company suddenly to announce low profits it would be a stronger story than a notorious loss-making concern revealing a small loss. PR people can manipulate expectations, preparing the ground for bad news with judicious briefing and leaking, even making things sound worse than they are. When the bad news finally emerges it is no longer news – and if the concern has been exaggerated there may even be some relief. On the other hand good news can sound even more impressive if expectations are managed downwards in advance. Journalists are willing participants because, either way, they are being offered exclusive stories.

*Creating alternative news.* If an organization is the subject of bad news and there are no major alternative stories around which would facilitate a news burial (see below) then PR people working for powerful, newsworthy organizations can sometimes create their own news in the form of decoy stories which distract the media. Rival news organizations which feel chagrined at missing the original story will often happily participate in this ploy.

*Complaints.* Bravado aside, no journalist likes being the subject of a serious, strongly expressed complaint. At the very least it makes the individual feel uneasy. But PR people's complaints sometimes ascend the chain of command. Well-placed and coordinated complaints to the journalist's editors and other members of the management team – even to proprietors and nonexecutive directors – can cause a media organization to hesitate or moderate its coverage.

*Threats.* Lurking in the background of most complaints is some kind of threat. Often this does not have to be expressed. The subtlety of this process, coupled to the fact that most of those involved seek to play it down, means that it will forever elude verifiable research. However a number of levers can be brought into play. One is the denial of future exclusives and assistance, with the implication that a competitor would benefit. Another may be the withdrawal of advertising. Frequently the threat of regulatory or legal action is used. Fear of the latter – typically the prospect of being sued for libel – is often enough to deter media organizations. Even if they are sure of their facts the media dread the uncertainty, as well as the costs and waste of resources, inherent in legal proceedings. The suggestion that legal action is in the offing can be used to deter rival news organizations, thereby halting the spread of the story. It is also possible, even in democracies, for governments to exploit their position as arbiters of media policy to cajole media organizations.

*Undermining hostile stories.* If negative stories nonetheless emerge in the media, a further array of PR tactics can be used to undermine and devalue them. The skill of the PR practitioner lies in knowing which combination of tactics to use and how to apply to them:

- An organization can swiftly acknowledge and, where appropriate, apologize for a problem, at the same time announcing measures to put things right. If it does so it often removes the story's sting – the tension between the organization and external opinion which is required to sustain a news story of this kind – and the coverage often peters out.

- The source of the story, be it an organization or an individual, can be attacked and discredited. Personalities are key ingredients in any news story, and if they lack credibility or appear ridiculous anything they say is undermined. Often PR people go one stage further, supplying an alternative source with equal or greater credibility that can be used to contradict or undermine the negative story.

- The credibility of the story can be undermined by focusing on inaccuracies, or elements in the story that cannot be corroborated. Journalists work at speed, and it is impossible for them to be experts on every facet of a big and complicated story, so it is a commonplace that big newspaper articles contain errors and weaknesses. Even if the central thrust of the story is correct, by highlighting faults and weak points PR people can cast doubt on the whole story.

- The problem can be made historic. By definition any report or investigation of an organization, however up to date, must relate to the past. It is a standard PR tactic to draw attention to this fact and stress that things have since changed for the better – an assertion that cannot be readily disproved.

- Problems can also be pushed away. Typically this involves setting up a review or inquiry, or commissioning a report, a response which normally looks sensible and responsible and is hard for critics to gainsay. Such a step can defuse the immediate crisis and it buys the organization time to refashion its approach to the issue. While the matter is under investigation journalists can simply be told that they will need to wait. Governments tend to be particularly keen on this technique.

- PR people will always seek to accentuate the positive. Even the most critical reports often contain positive aspects which can be seized upon and emphasized in press statements and interviews.

Even if an apology is called for, much more time can be devoted to talking about good news and what went right. If expectations have been managed properly ahead of a bad news story (see above) PR people may be able to trade on news which is good only in a relative sense – for example, criticisms that are milder than anticipated.

- The media can be starved of fresh material. News stories need replenishment if they are to be kept going as journalists cannot keep recycling the same facts. If the organization at the center of a media storm refuses to provide additional information and, importantly, refuses to make spokespeople available for interview, the news furor often dies down.

- Journalistic and media rivalries can be exploited. All media outlets have a vested interest in undermining – where possible – their competitors' stories. A number of the tactics described above – for example the undermining of sources and stories, and the planting of decoy stories – depend on making use of such rivalries. Often individual journalists will help PR people use the tactics described above, spurred on by the prospect of getting their own stories.

The tactics described above have to be used with caution by PR practitioners. Adopting a tough stance with the media may be necessary but stores up resentments, which can come back to haunt PR people when their organization is vulnerable. Ultimately such behavior is judged on whether it is seen as a legitimate action in the interests of the organization, which does not endanger or disadvantage the public; or on whether it is seen as designed to protect an organization that is at fault and has avoided taking proper remedial action and responsibility for the alleged crisis or problem. Journalists and PR people and their clients often disagree on whether the end has justified the means.

## The importance of timing

When PR people want maximum coverage for their stories, they "sell" them when the news is in short supply and the market is less competitive. Government and commercial activity tends to slow down at weekends, when offices are closed and fewer announcements are made, but the media still requires a supply of raw material for Mondays. This has given rise to "Sunday-for-Monday" stories, whereby PR people seek to exploit the lower threshold for newsworthiness. Similar opportunities exist during holiday periods, again caused by the dearth of normal news.

The reverse is true when PR people are obliged to announce something which does not reflect well on their organizations and where the ideal outcome would be as little coverage as possible. Skilled PR people then wait until there is a glut of news – perhaps one big event which is dominating the media or a series of big stories – to release their "bad news," in the hope that it will be ignored or covered only perfunctorily. Sometimes major news stories can be anticipated, and so the release of "bad news" can be planned, but the opportunity also arises when an unforeseen event or disaster occurs.

---

**A good day to bury bad news**

On September 11, 2001 – 9/11 – as the twin towers were attacked in New York, Jo Moore was working as a "spin doctor" for a British government department that had nothing to do with the events across the Atlantic. She was following the huge unfolding story and spotted an opportunity. Her department needed to make an announcement about local politicians' expenses. The news was – mildly – controversial, and she wanted it to receive minimal attention. She emailed colleagues that it was "a very good day to get out anything we want to bury."

This only became public because she used email – rather than a deniable conversation – and her words were leaked to the media by colleagues. Her remark was deemed extremely insensitive and caused a media storm in the United Kingdom, forcing Moore to apologize. Moore was finally forced to resign from government in 2002 following further allegations that she had wanted to "bury" more bad news by announcing it on the day of Princess Margaret's funeral.[22]

All journalists are slaves to deadlines, the exact times when they have to submit their stories for publication or broadcast, and effective PR people know this and factor it into their calculations. It is hard to overstate the tyranny of the deadline – after all, once it is missed the news is useless to the journalist concerned and competitive advantage potentially passes to any other media outlet. This can be exploited in two ways by the PR industry. If the story being sold is *not* major news – something that is true of most positive news stories and which hence applies to most of what PR people try to place in the media – then supplying it to journalists well in advance is a good idea. Journalists want time to prepare their stories, and when they are close to their deadlines they are under pressure and reluctant to bother with new material.

If the story is much bigger and irresistible the calculation is more complicated. Sometimes it can still be advantageous to give the media plenty of time to prepare their stories, particularly if the story is strongly positive or a particular media outlet is being given an exclusive. But PR people may also deliberately choose to keep journalists in the dark right up to their deadlines. This reflects their awareness that journalists have to cover really major stories as soon as they occur – to the point that newspapers will publish extra editions and broadcasters will break into bulletins or run special programs. If the journalists are right up against their deadlines they have little choice but to cover the story on the PR person's terms, as they lack time to seek alternative information or views.

Government press conferences are often considered to make for boring television, but during recent wars the key press conferences have frequently been timed to coincide with the start of important news programs. In particular US military press conferences from the Middle East have been scheduled with the timing of key news programs back in the United States in mind.

In the scale of news values, war is deemed of the utmost importance by broadcasters. They feel obliged to report all developments instantly and are often obliged to cover such press conferences live. Thus news and images of important events reaches audiences via the mass media, but with little scope for mediation by journalists.

Timing is also crucial to attempts to suppress bad news. In the 24/7 rolling news environment which has emerged in recent years information spreads very quickly, and major news stories can be endlessly repeated within minutes of their emergence, leaving an indelible mark on the reputation of individuals and organizations. Ideally PR people seek to act before bad news emerges, but failing that they have to be able to tackle stories instantly and rebut them before the mud sticks.

## The Beckhams and the "sex-mad PR beauty":[23] the ultimate PR tale for our times?

In April 2004 the British footballer David Beckham, who now plays for LA Galaxy, found himself in the midst of a storm in the newspaper press. Beckham's celebrity status as an international footballer (he was then captain of the England football team, played for Real Madrid, and had formerly played for Manchester United) was matched by that of his popstar wife, the former Spice Girl Victoria Beckham or Posh Spice. One former newspaper editor turned professor of journalism was to describe what happened as the UK's biggest tabloid story for a decade.[24]

Ostensibly the story had nothing to do with PR. It concerned unproven allegations that, while in Spain, Beckham had had an extramarital affair with a young woman, Rebecca Loos. Beckham has always denied the allegations, describing them as "ludicrous." However in practice the story oozed PR from every pore, and hence highlights some of the PR practices which shape our media.

### *"PR girl"*

Rebecca Loos herself was, according to many newspaper accounts, a "PR Girl," although the term was often used interchangeably with PA or personal assistant, underlining the problems of deciding who is or is not a PR person. It was suggested that she was prompted to talk by the fact that a rearrangement of the Beckhams' PR had led to her losing her job. However fair or unfair using PR to describe her duties might be, it certainly seemed to be a useful way of describing a young woman whose working life involved consorting with celebrities. PR was, in the tabloid world, firmly associated with sex and fun: "the sports PR girl had forged a reputation for sexual impropriety"[25]

... "it all began with the bisexual PR girl buttering up David's WIFE Victoria."[26] A former boyfriend not only compared her to *Sex and the City*'s Samantha Jones but claimed that Loos saw the resemblance too, adding that when they watched the show together she would say "That's me."[27]

The newspapers described Loos as leading a party-strewn life between major capital cities and enjoying affairs with leading tennis players, while helping David Beckham to settle down in Madrid and assisting his wife in her alleged attempts to get discounts at leading stores. There was little sense of her using the special skills PR people like to claim for themselves. However according to an old school friend, "She is typically Dutch – very open and a 'people person' – which is probably why she went into PR. It's what I imagine she would be very good at."[28]

### PR machines lock horns

*The Max factor*

> In this game of master-manipulation, the winner takes all.[29]

As the story unfolded one of Britain's most famous PR people, Max Clifford, emerged as a major player, featuring in dozens of articles as a "PR guru," a "PR mastermind,"[30] the "eminence grise of the kiss and tell market."[31]

From the outset Clifford is identified as the man behind the story – the person who sold it – but the details remained unconfirmed and murky. This aspect of Clifford's PR practice is distinct from the common understanding of PR, in that selling stories to the media for a commission is not generally seen as part of PR's remit. Nonetheless, although the newspapers were reluctant to admit it, their reliance on PR for a huge story was laid bare.

Clifford's involvement went further than simply acting as a broker for Loos. He became one of a variety of PR people invited to comment on the story – demonstrating that as PR and spin become an increasing talking point the media approaches PR people for expert comment. He was able to offer his views as a participant, with both he and the tabloids applying a whiff of subterfuge and a hint of menace: "Last night PR guru Max Clifford repeated his warning,"[32] or "There's more clouds gathering."[33]

By later in the week Clifford was seen visiting the offices of *The Sun*, the UK's best-selling daily paper, causing a leading politician to wait in line while he conferred with the newspaper's editor.[34] Following the meeting fresh revelations appeared on the front page of the paper, together with a tribute to Clifford from the grateful newspaper. He was now described as a "famed PR super-guru." *The Sun* added: "Take any number of agenda-setting stories from the past two decades and Clifford's name will appear time and time again."[35]

Thus Clifford emerges as a master-manipulator, a spider exerting power at the center of a media web. Even if his exact role is hard to pin down, he seems to be in control of events and indispensable to the media.

### The Beckhams' fightback

Rebecca Loos may have sold her story when her PR company was allegedly spurned by the Beckhams, but that still left no fewer than three PR companies in charge of their image,[36] putting a focus on the scale of the PR resources employed by a modern celebrity couple. Initially the efforts of their "hapless PR machine" were not viewed favorably. Two days after the revelations first appeared "happy family" photographs of the Beckhams were published, but were seen by many as part of an empty and cynical "PR counteroffensive." A *Daily Mirror* headline told readers "Marriage is not just PR,"[37] and *The Times* referred to the Beckhams' Faustian pact with the media.[38] Even Rebecca Loos spoke about the Beckhams' PR efforts as she "savaged the increasingly desperate PR stunts by the tarnished golden couple last week, branding them a 'crass charade'."[39] As this shows, newspapers assume an awareness of the use of PR on the part of their readers, and readily use terms like "PR stunt" as shorthand for activities that are devoid of real substance or meaning and are only designed to obtain the right kind of publicity.

A final twist to the PR struggle was *The Sun*'s suggestion that had the Beckhams hired Max Clifford themselves the story might not have appeared.[40] This reference to PR's usually hidden role in suppressing news stories further embellished Clifford's reputation for wielding power behind the scenes. However using the model of the information marketplace (see p. 33) it is hard to see how Clifford could have achieved this. The main reason for choosing not to use a story of this kind would be because of the promise of an even better one – and given the scale of the story this would have been almost impossible to achieve.

### "Brand Beckham"

"Serious" newspapers sought to excuse their coverage of the Beckham story by portraying the PR struggle as a news story in its own right, and debating its implications for the reputation of Brand Beckham (BB), reflecting the Beckhams' heavy involvement in product endorsement for companies such as Gillette and Tesco. The day after the initial story appeared *The Times* was citing PR experts on the possible damage to David Beckham's "untainted image, which generates tens of millions of pounds each year."[41] Other reports highlighted concerns for Victoria Beckham's brand image. As "Top PR guru" Ian Monk commented in the *Mail* on Sunday, "Of course, the whole BB myth is based on a shallow but superbly cultivated perception, a brilliantly sophisticated trick of modern image that remained flawless until the rumble in Madrid." In Monk's view, the affair had shifted power back to the corporate sponsors and the Beckhams' PR would be directed at assuaging their concerns. (Notwithstanding this, years later Brand Beckham remains in good health.)[42]

### The future of an abusive relationship

Where is the relationship between PR and journalists heading? Journalism retains latent strengths. It has the last word – PR lacks a public voice other than the one it finds through journalism. Journalists undoubtedly preserve some independence, and powerful media organizations cannot be easily pushed around. Investigative journalism may be under threat but is not extinct. No PR person, even those working for the most powerful organizations, can be wholly certain about how their organization or client will be reported: as we have seen, coverage can be massaged, but it cannot be fully controlled. In recent years all governments in developed countries have received hostile coverage from time to time, as have many business leaders and major companies.

The journalist Nick Davies laments the state of his craft in his book *Flat Earth News*. As we have seen, he paints a picture of an industry increasingly denuded of resources and outgunned by the ascendant discipline of PR.

He claims that "almost all journalists across the whole developed world now work within a kind of professional cage which distorts their work and crushes their spirit" and that his is "a corrupted profession." [43] Although he casts around for cures, he says that he is "taking a snapshot of a cancer" and he fears "the illness is terminal." [44]

But increasingly even negative stories in reality reflect PR battles fought between rival organizations (and sometimes dissident PR *within* organizations): the media simply report and comment upon on the conflict. As they do so they review the rival qualities of the PR. Journalists perform the not unimportant role of judges when summing up at the end of the court case: they summarize the evidence advanced by PR people, and point to its strengths and weaknesses. They also offer their own opinions. Occasionally they will be able to go further than this – but this is the exception rather than the rule. Journalists and others are aware of this and frequently rue their growing impotence. They argue for more and better journalism and point hopefully to the exceptions to the rule.

For the most part these debates are sterile, long on diagnosis and short on realistic ideas for a cure, and represent so much whistling in the wind. However praiseworthy the objective there is no chance of it being realized. Talking up sporadic examples of journalistic vigor does not affect the underlying economic reality. Nor are new media necessarily able to rescue old media. Blogs and citizen journalism are interesting phenomena but cannot be a solution to the problems which so many journalists decry. Some exponents of digital media may be popular; most are not. As news-gatherers they have not been able to match the resources, training, and experience of traditional media, and the new digital products are themselves susceptible to PR. The market pressures are inexorable: journalism is going to continue to struggle for resources.

PR, on the other hand, is awash with resources. But rather than simply recoiling in horror at this, critics should pause and consider whether what has occurred is necessarily a bad thing. Healthy debate is actually fostered by public relations because PR is ubiquitous: charities and campaigning organizations employ PR to savage companies and governments, and, more subtly, their own competitors in the not-for-profit sector; rival companies sometimes use PR to attack each other; and political parties do the same all the time. The debate will never be perfectly balanced – what debate is? – but neither was journalism ever able to report the world perfectly. The rise of PR may be unstoppable but it is not necessarily harmful. Indeed, given that journalism is unlikely to recover its past resources, the current paradox is that the best hope for the media and for informed debate may be more PR for more voices.

# CHAPTER 4

# The lying game

## PR – the truth and other ethical issues

> I stand up and say that an important part of public relations is lies and deceit. We all know that but they won't ever admit it.[1]

In 2007, in conjunction with *PR Week*, the authors organized a debate at the University of Westminster on the motion "PR has a duty to tell the truth." Over three hundred people – PR students from all over the world and UK-based PR practitioners – attended the event in central London. After an hour and a half of lively discussion, with plenty of interventions from the floor, the motion was voted down by a narrow margin: the audience concluded that PR people did *not* have a duty to tell the truth.

This was not the first or last time that this issue has been or will be debated in PR circles. The issue remains one which finds raw nerves in the PR industry. Our debate attracted a great deal of comment around the world in the blogosphere. Later that year the authors took opposing sides in a restaging of the debate in front of an audience of students at the Sorbonne in Paris. The French result was even more conclusive, with an overwhelming vote against the motion.

Max Clifford, author of the outburst at the top of this page, has taken part in many of these debates, opposing the notion that there is a duty to tell the truth. He is the *bete noire* of the UK's PR industry (although – but perhaps also because – he is one of the few practitioners to be widely known outside PR circles). His work and his client-base is distinctive and his perspective may not be the same as that of main-stream PR people, but his words encapsulate the contrast between "we," pragmatic PR people who might admit to lying but generally keep their heads down and get on with their jobs, and "they," PR idealists who publicly deny it. "They" is shorthand for the official face of PR: an overlapping grouping of past and present office hold-ers in PR's trade bodies, PR educators, and authors of books about PR. Such people may be few in number, and sometimes limited in their business experience, but they are normally the only people to put their views on the record: most PR people lack the time or inclination. Understandably few PR practitioners want to put their heads above the parapet and admit to lying – the subtleties of the argument are too easily lost upon clients and employers. However a former press secre-tary to a long-serving British Prime Minister, who outranks most in terms of PR experience, put it as follows:

> Sometimes, press secretaries have to be more than economical with the truth; they have to dispense with it altogether for what they perceive to be the greater good.[2]

It is easy to see why some PR people should get exercised about this issue, and the requirement to tell the truth features prominently in most of the many codes of ethics produced by the PR industry's trade bodies. No-one likes to be accused of being a liar, and yet, as we have seen, PR people are frequently the subject of abuse of this kind from journalists. As we shall also explain, PR is often associated with propaganda, with all its negative resonances, and "official" PR has struggled hard to distance itself. Insisting on strict adherence to the truth is often seen as a way of establishing a clear dividing line between the two. Finally, the portrayal of PR in popular culture is very influential – a recurring theme of this book – and novels, films, and television series often highlight PR's ambiguous relationship with the truth. Readers might immediately think of recent portray-als of cynical spin-doctors and PR people for whom the truth is not a priority, but the tradition is much more deeply rooted than that.

In 1940 Frank Pick, Director of the Ministry of Information, clashed with Britain's wartime Prime Minister Winston Churchill:

*Churchill*: I understand you object to the dropping of leaflets.

*Pick*: Yes – what is written is not wholly true and that is bad propaganda.

*Churchill*: This is no time to be concerned with the niceties.

*Pick*: I have never told a lie in my life.

*Churchill*: Yesterday the Germans shelled Dover with their long-range guns. This afternoon I shall be visiting Dover. I may be killed by a German shell. If so, it will be a great comfort to me to know that on the last day of my life I spoke with a man who had never told a lie in his life. Get out.

Pick was dismissed shortly afterwards and died the following year.[3]

## Lovable rogues

Perhaps the best gloss that can be put on depictions of this aspect of PR is that PR people are lovable rogues, prepared to step beyond the bounds of the truth but with charm and *élan*, in a way that is ultimately harmless. Before the Second World War, in the musical *Waikiki Wedding*, Bing Crosby's Hawaii-based PR man launches a great tradition when he simulates a volcanic eruption, engineers a mock attack on someone in the street, and even gets a woman to impersonate his mother. However these acts are portrayed as ingenious and amusing examples of sleight of hand, and not as serious or malicious.

Another big star vehicle from prewar Hollywood, *Four's a Crowd*, does the same. Errol Flynn's character, who actually calls himself a PR man – the first such example we have been able to find – uses his sharp wits with cheerful and stylish amorality to secure an important client. His wooing of his millionaire prospect includes making pretend love to the potential client's granddaughter; resuming the editorship of the newspaper for which he formerly worked in order to launch a campaign of vilification against the potential client – and then offering himself up as a PR savior; and ingratiating himself with his potential client by posing as a fellow model-railway enthusiast and then buttering the tracks in order to win a train race. He even engages in amorous conversations with two women simultaneously over the telephone. As his journalist bride-to-be says of him: "You play hopscotch from one doublecross to another."

However this is done with great good humor, and as is the case with *Waikiki Wedding*, a PR person's work provides an excellent peg upon which to hang a farce about working life. The victims of

Errol Flynn's PR man bear no grudges, and he ultimately marries his journalist fiancée and sparring partner. The only harbinger of a darker, more serious future is the voice of Hermann, the PR man's German immigrant barber and the only European voice in an otherwise all-American film. He displays real indignation in his imperfect English after Flynn's character describes his work:

> You call that public relationships. I call that bamboozling the peoples – and I am the peoples and if I am not I'm rather quit than I don't want your blood money.

## Double dealers

In postwar America the issue of the truth and its relationship with PR was treated more earnestly. The novel and film *The Man in a Gray Flannel Suit* are meditations upon the moral compromises of corporate life in 1950s New York, seen through the dilemmas faced by PR man played by yet another Hollywood big name. Gregory Peck's character enters PR for the money, and his subsequent career is contrasted with wartime service as a paratrooper, with the latter serving as a yardstick of integrity. At the outset he tells his wife that "I might as well get used to this doubletalk from the beginning … I'm good at tackling honesty, but I have an idea that things are going to be a little more complicated."

She is sickened, and finally says:

> The real idea was that I wanted you to go out and fight for something again … For a decent man there's never any peace of mind without honesty … how long it'll be before you think it'll be simpler and safer not to tell me the truth?

Another 1950s film, the classic *film noir*, *Sweet Smell of Success*, explores similar issues amid the seedy milieu of New York's press agents and gossip columnists (illustrating why PR people had become keen on distinguishing themselves from press agents and publicists).[4] One client tells the anti-hero press agent played by Tony Curtis: "You're a liar Sidney. Oh, it's a publicity man's nature to be a liar. I wouldn't hire you if you wasn't a liar."

The all-powerful gossip columnist with whom the press agent is locked into a relationship of mutual dependence says much the same, describing his counterpart as "a man of forty faces not one, none too pretty and all deceptive ... a hungry press agent and fully up to all the tricks of his very slimy trade."

## The truth debate continues[5]

In contemporary films and television series there is less focus on the extent to which PR people deceive others, reflecting the fact that the outside world is now more used to the existence of the PR industry and unsurprised that PR people do not tell the whole truth and nothing but the truth. The gap between the PR person's words and reality remains – *AbFab*'s Edina Monsoon makes "the crap into credible" – but the issue no longer seems to shock and is not dwelt upon. This acceptance is probably why the uproar caused by the outcome of our debate in 2007 was confined to PR circles.

The Church of England's Director of Communications commented: "I was dismayed. Truth and integrity have to be the cornerstone of our profession if we are to have any credibility with the media and the outside world." Meanwhile the President of Europe's largest PR organization, the Chartered Institute of Public Relations, urged his membership to take advantage of an on-line poll to reverse the verdict of the debate and "uphold our Code and the integrity of the industry."[6] Other PR people from around the world who commented were "disappointed," "very disappointed," "shocked," "shocked and appalled," "genuinely stunned," and "gob smacked." For others it was "deeply worrying," "incredibly depressing," a "shocking indictment"; "no-one adheres to a moral code anymore and that's sad and destructive." An American PR "thought our friends across the pond ate some bad fish and chips," while a scandalized Argentinean blogger referred readers to the pronouncements of the Roman Catholic Church's Pontifical Council on Social Communications. The surprise about the debate's outcome reveals an intriguing lack of self-knowledge on the part of the industry.

But the vote failed wider tests of newsworthiness. A well-known journalist and blogger thought people shouldn't be "*too* surprised," while a US newspaper editor thought the arguments of the anti-truth side rang true, based on his experience of the PR industry, and was only surprised that the outcome of the vote should be so close.

For PR people opposed to lying the main planks to their argument are more practical than moral. They argue that what might suffice in the world of celebrities and entertainment – the world which Hollywood publicists and Max Clifford personify – would not pass muster in the world of serious, corporate public relations where companies have to consider their long-term reputations. Linked to this is the notion that an organization's interests can never be best served by telling lies because, if and when the truth emerges, the credibility of the PR person and the organization they serve will be fatally damaged. These are of course not moral arguments but matters of expedience, leaving people tempted to lie if they feel they can get away with it. They come perilously close to Goebbels' line of reasoning: that in the long run lies were usually the stupidest and least effective form of publicity.[7]

The final argument was even more pragmatic: debating the issue was harmful to PR and should therefore be avoided. As Peter Hehir, the former Chairman of Porter Novelli International and erstwhile President of the international trade body the International Communications Consultancy Organization (ICCO), put it, "How depressing that people have the time and inclination to take part in such ridiculous debates," going on to argue that an institutional memory panel of senior practitioners might help the industry to stop harming itself. One cynical PR blogger took this to its logical conclusion: "I think PR has shot itself in the foot. It could do with appointing a PR firm to limit the damage, lie a little and put PR in a positive spin."

For outsiders the notion that PR people have a duty to tell the truth is unconvincing, and PR people's protestations to the contrary sound shrill and unconvincing – in fact they are so unconvincing that they raise further questions about PR practitioners' honesty and are actually counterproductive. Many recognize that people in all walks of life have to lie in order to get on with their lives. Few apply Immanuel Kant's absolute opposition to lying to their day-to-day lives – famously, for Kant, if a murderer was looking for a child, it would be wrong to point the murderer in a false direction. In practice people make exceptions and compromise. This is true for journalists as well as PR people. In a recent book the BBC political journalist and former newspaper editor Andrew Marr highlighted this:

> Try, just for a day, a policy of absolute honesty. You think the neighbours are dreary or obese? For God's sake don't hide it. You find your daughter wittering? Tell her – never mind the tears. Your boss has a bad body odour problem? Tell the brute as frankly as you inhale it. A day of honesty would be enough to finish most of us.[8]

PR's particular problem arises from its symbiotic relationship with the news media, coupled to the fact that only one side in the relationship normally has a public voice: the media. It is like hearing an account of a troubled marriage from one partner. Journalists like to see themselves as intrepid seekers after the truth, and often regard PR people as obstacles as they go about their investigations. The PR perspective is different. They know that for journalists bad news is normally preferable to good news, and arguments have a higher news value than agreement. This puts PR in an invidious position. All organizations suffer from problems or experience disputes, but to tell the full truth about such matters all the time would be to invite a tidal wave of hostile news coverage. The life expectancy of any organization which answered all enquiries about difficulties and disagreements with absolute honesty would be very brief. Indeed, journalists are often quick to criticize politicians or company spokespeople as naive or inexperienced when they are rash enough to express a truly honest opinion on a controversial issue.

Obfuscation is sometimes possible, but refusing to say anything – thereby avoiding lying – is a tactic of limited use as refusing to comment tends to lend credence to allegations.

*The Sun* is the UK's best selling daily newspaper, with a circulation of around 3 million a day. It is famous for its lively front page headlines. One of the most famous examples dates from 1986 and has become the stuff of legend. It read as follows:

### FREDDIE STARR ATE MY HAMSTER

Freddie Starr was a British celebrity, a well-known comedian. The story was provided to *The Sun* by Max Clifford, and is one of the most famous episodes in the celebrity PR man's long career of supplying material to popular newspapers. However no-one ever seriously suggested that this story – despite its brilliant, memorable headline – is true. But it was the kind of story people want to read. We suspect *The Sun*'s journalists knew this before they went to print. The story illustrates the fact that while journalists talk the talk of crusading for truth, they know that they are also in the entertainment business, a line of work where PR people can be useful suppliers.[9]

This reality is understood by all participants in the media relations business – indeed it is so well understood that it rarely arouses comment. Public figures in business or politics are seldom labeled as liars for denying that they are at loggerheads with their colleagues, or for refusing to admit problems and – when this becomes untenable – minimizing the scale of the problems. Appearing united is essential to the long-term survival of any organization, however much disunity there may be. Organizations also have to present themselves as confident: if they are experiencing obvious difficulties they must appear positive and in control of events (although this may not be the case). As a rule of thumb, whenever an organization speaks of its full confidence in an employee whose behavior has been called into question this is less than true: the only reason the organization does so is because that confidence is in doubt.

Such "lies," which is what they technically are, are the small change of media relations work. Journalists do not consider the perpetrators to be liars, because they accept that PR people are in the business of presenting their paymasters in best possible light, minimizing the negative and accentuating the positive. No-one should rely solely on an organization's PR person if they want to know the full truth about it. Thus information exchanged in this context is discounted, and often contains socially acceptable "soft" lies, "white lies," the sort of thing we all say. This is expected and should be distinguished from "hard" lies – the conscious dissemination of incorrect facts and figures about important matters. This is seldom deemed acceptable, is sometimes even illegal, and, if revealed, rebounds on the perpetrator.

One of the authors handled the launch of one of the UK's largest online banks. Prelaunch secrecy was vital as the new bank wanted to maximize its competitive advantage by maintaining control over the timing of the announcement. However, as is often the case, a journalist heard about the preparations and rang up to enquire.

Telling the truth would have meant losing control over the announcement before the bank was ready, leaving competitors a free hand. Nor was obfuscation or refusal to comment an option: the journalist had the germ of a story and if the main thrust of it was not denied it was likely that it would be published in some form. The option chosen was to tell a direct lie. The journalist was told that the new facilities were simply a new back office for the bank's conventional branch network: untrue, but effective and harmless.

## PR ethics

The issue of lying often heads the charge sheet when critics vilify the PR industry, but is only one of a series of ethical issues which constantly bubble to the surface when people discuss PR. These concerns are reflected in "official" PR's many codes of conduct, although as we shall see elsewhere there has never been much scope for proper enforcement of these codes. The concerns of outsiders can be broken down under two main headings: the nature of the people and organizations served by PR; and the techniques used.

### *The special forces of capitalism*

PR has always been associated with big business. It came into being in its modern form a hundred years ago to manage the relationship between corporations and the emerging mass media – and beyond that the public. It follows that people who do not like or are suspicious of capitalism do not like or are suspicious of PR. Indeed many attacks on PR are really thinly disguised attacks on the business world. If advertising is pilloried as the public face of capitalism, PR practitioners and lobbyists are often seen as the sinister special forces of the big corporations and their allies in government, operating behind enemy lines and using a variety of unfair, clandestine tricks. The mystery which envelops PR is a source of fascination, and some PR people contribute to this by reveling in and cultivating an aura of power and a sense of mystique. For people who have had difficulty accepting the triumph of capitalism in the ideological wars of the twentieth century and for whom conspiracy theories offer some sense of relief for their feelings of impotence and despair, PR is a good target. As one of the pioneers of media studies put it: "The rise of PR [represents] the direct control by private or state interests of the flow of public information in the interest, not of rational discourse, but of manipulation."[10]

Objecting to PR on the basis of the causes it serves leads into a *cul de sac*. PR can serve the interests of any company, large or small, from the most hated multinational to innocuous local businesses or indeed wholesalers and others who have little contact with the public: unless one repudiates business altogether it is hard to object to the use of PR *per se*. Typically therefore people object to the use of PR in particular, unpopular business sectors. The problem with this approach is that no two people can agree on which businesses are acceptable and which are not – and even one's individual perceptions can alter over time or in response to particular events.

This can be readily illustrated. Some might object to the arms industry altogether on pacifist grounds, and one major PR agency head in the United Kingdom boasted that he would never work for an arms company.[11] More might object to the sale of particular kinds of weapons, or arms sales to particular regimes, but be unable to reach a consensus on which weapons and which regimes are acceptable. However some might see providing arms, for example to fight a tyrannical dictator, as deeply moral. Even those who object outright to arms sales are caught in a trap, due to the interconnected nature of the business world: companies that do not make weapons themselves may be supplying goods and services to those that do.

Or take the growing consensus about climate change and the threat of global warming. General agreement about the problem does not mean that there is much common ground about solutions. Some urge more use of nuclear power, others strongly oppose it. Some favor wind farms, others disagree. Some back the use of biofuels, while others see this as counterproductive. Tree planting to offset air travel is fashionable in some circles, but is not backed by some of the largest environmental groups. Encouraging food exports from developing countries may seem uncontroversial, but what about the air miles which accrue when they are flown to marketplaces in the developed world? In the case of the environment even if people can agree on a destination, they rarely agree on the route to it. The list of controversial businesses and moral dilemmas is endless. From gambling to tobacco, from alcohol to unhealthy foods, from pornography to advertising directed at children, most people have ethical qualms about some legal forms of business activity.

In their role as messengers for the world of business PR people are sucked into all these and other debates: if you hate the particular business or business sector you will detest its PR. The reality is that business and PR are *amoral*. Business may create the wealth which we all need to survive, but it does so by serving human needs and desires, and few would claim that all human desires – or even the ways in which some humans satisfy their needs – are moral. In its role as the servant of business PR deploys a set of techniques which can be used for any cause, good or bad. While there is no evidence that PR people are more or less moral than others, there is always a temptation to align one's morals with one's business instincts. For example, one's point of view on whether biofuels are a good thing might be influenced by the prospect of well-rewarded work from a biofuel company, even if one tries hard to convince oneself that one has reached the decision independently!

> A principle is not a principle until it costs you money.
> Bill Bernbach, American adman[12]

So much for business, but of course much PR activity is associated with other areas of life. Here similar problems apply. Few would argue that governments are necessarily ethical or moral in their intentions or actions, and so political PR is forever open to ethical questioning. Once again, there is a temptation to be self-serving, and find arguments to support the cause of any government or political organization for which one is working, while lambasting opponents. This is understandable, but not particularly moral. Likewise the not-for-profit sector. Charities and campaigning organizations, from international brands such as Greenpeace and Amnesty International to millions of smaller, little-known local examples, deploy considerable PR muscle, as we shall see. However the causes they espouse are the product of personal opinions and value judgments, however widely shared, and often contradict those of other not-for-profit organizations. And once again, even if the destination is agreed, the route to it is often disputed.

The righteousness of the causes served by PR may be forever open to doubt, but the techniques used ought to be easier to pin down. This is what the numerous codes to which many PR practitioners sign up focus on, although as we shall see they have proved all but impossible to enforce. In practice the use of controversial PR techniques is tempered more effectively by social pressure and the expectations of individual marketplaces around the world. PR people who overstep the boundaries of what is deemed acceptable in a particular set of circumstances risk losing the standing they need in order to operate effectively. PR is in the end a profoundly social activity, and lack of social acceptance – at least within the desired circles – renders the PR person useless.

PR people face additional vigilance from the media, and from some other external sources. The fact that tracking and monitoring PR requires knowledge and effort means that it is not an obvious target in the way that advertising is, but at the same time this makes it particularly appealing to the critical cognoscenti and those who believe in conspiracy theories. The machinations of corporate and political PR are the stuff of specialist websites such as www.prwatch. org, the extensive, professionally staffed PR monitoring service run by the Center for Media and Democracy in the United States, whose founders have authored a series of widely available books of which the best known is probably *Toxic Sludge is Good for You*; and www.spinwatch.org, a newer UK equivalent.

Ultimately there is much more gray than black and white in the field of PR ethics. As we observed earlier, whether the ends justify the PR means always depends on what you think of the ends.

# CHAPTER 5

# Portrait of an industry

## Money, motives, and mergers

The PR industry's activities are notoriously hard to quantify. Fortunately, many of the reasons that make it difficult to measure the PR industry's dimensions have the unexpected benefit of illuminating some of the industry's characteristics.

The biggest barrier to producing accurate statistics about the PR industry is probably the fact that, as we describe elsewhere, PR is not a proper profession with restricted entry. You do not need to register anywhere in order to be able to practice PR. Consequently trade associations and professional bodies only represent a minority of those who work in the industry. The number of people who work in PR but are not members of one of these bodies remains a matter of speculation.

Another factor is that many practitioners are anxious to free themselves from some of the negative perceptions of PR and want to describe what they do in ways likely to enhance their status and income. As a result they describe themselves as almost anything but PR people: they are corporate reputation managers, campaigners, communication strategists, employer brand consultants, creative directors, or corporate social responsibility specialists. A quick look at advertisements for jobs in the sector will reveal a myriad of titles. Who should be counted in and who counted out?

There are also problems – discussed in Chapter 7 – with defining PR and its overlaps with other marketing communication disciplines. Are events organizers, and newsletter and website copywriters, involved in aspects of PR? Often they are, but if one included all such people in the PR headcount the numbers would balloon out of recognition.

Finally, there is the way the business is structured. Most PR people work in-house but are scattered in penny packets across many thousands of organizations, most of which employ only one or two PR staff. Only the largest organizations employ many more, and the picture is blurred by the issues described above. Charting the consultancy side of the business poses similar problems. Despite the emergence of large international marketing groups, the majority of consultancies are still very small. Indeed even the big consultancies seldom have more than 200 staff in a single country. For example, according to O'Dwyer's in the United States, in 2006 only the top five of the 140 largest independent PR firms with major US operations had over 200 staff.[1] Most of the top 140 had staff numbers well below 30. The vast majority of the thousands of PR firms in the United States probably have fewer than ten staff; plenty will have just one. Many of these small firms – or individuals who may simply be freelancing – come and go, expand and contract, merge with other firms, or change their names with great speed. So producing a precise map of the industry remains problematic.

PR's split identity – both in-house PR and consultancy PR are substantial business specializations in their own right – is in contrast to other marketing services. Advertising has always been and remains essentially an external agency function, reflecting the fact that even the biggest advertisers have seldom been able or willing to recruit and retain high quality advertising talent to work in-house. Marketing on the other hand is traditionally a core "in-house" function of a business, and is seen as an indispensable part of a business's day-to-day functioning. PR's unusual status suggests that the rationales for external advertising and in-house marketing both apply to PR.

## The consultancy sector

PR consultancy was born in the United States about one hundred years ago. There was already a well-established tradition of press agents creating publicity in the newspaper press for circuses and other forms of entertainment. But the emergence of huge businesses created a need for proactive public relations to build favorable impressions and boost consumption, and for reactive PR to handle the crises caused by strikes and corporate malpractice. Specialists in dealing with the rapidly emerging mass media inevitably began to emerge. Some of these specialists, such as Ivy Lee, Edward Bernays and, later, John W. Hill of what became Hill & Knowlton, realized there was more money to be made, and perhaps more interest to be had, through advising several organizations rather than just one.[2]

Many of the early PR consultancies were essentially cottage industries, built around individual personalities (they often bore the names of their founders, and some of these linger on). They were akin in size to the multitude of small PR firms which still make up much of the industry, as at this stage the owner (usually a man) employed only a handful of staff, and had a direct hand in most important client business. In the mid-twentieth century some of these small businesses grew into big companies, at least by the standards of the PR industry, such as Hill & Knowlton and Burson-Marsteller. They began to expand overseas, particularly in the United Kingdom where PR was slowly taking off.

By the 1980s, with President Reagan in power in the United States and Margaret Thatcher in the United Kingdom, businesses, the organizations most likely and able to pay for PR, had achieved ascendancy over ideas of big government and state ownership. The PR consultancy industry, particularly in the United Kingdom, started to grow at an unprecedented pace. This spurt of growth has been ascribed to the privatization policies pursued by Conservative governments in the 1980s.[3] Larger firms were well placed to benefit from the sale of state assets and they and other firms then developed further business links with the newly privatized businesses. (This pattern has more recently been repeated across formerly communist controlled Eastern Europe.)

The 1980s also saw a consumer boom and the emergence of the IT industry and Silicon Valley (which manifested itself in the emergence of a number of specialist IT consultancies). PR consultancies both made possible, and responded to, the growth in the media which occurred at the same time: the extra pages and supplements in the newspaper press and the rise of new magazines. They played an important part in the linked rise of celebrity culture but also benefited from it as journalists came to rely on them for their celebrity stories.

This boom allowed the PR consultancy sector – or at least its more successful constituents – to mature from cottage industries to boutiques, and from boutiques to fully fledged international businesses. High-profile individual personalities continued to play an important role but were now backed by teams of more senior and higher caliber staff, PR was increasingly becoming a graduate occupation, belatedly catching up with advertising, although at this stage few entrants would have studied PR. Consultancies adopted a more formal structure and were now capable of dealing with substantial client business without reference to the founder and owner. Senior staff continued to have a range of backgrounds, many having started their careers outside PR.

By the late 1990s PR consultancy sector was starting to take its current shape. The once dominant, high-profile personalities had for the most part left the firms they founded, having sold them to a series of large, international marketing services conglomerates. The remaining senior and experienced staff found themselves increasingly divorced from client work and instead forced to manage what were now large businesses. This change of emphasis led to many senior consultants quitting the new leviathans and establishing small consultancies offering strategic advice.

## The emergence of PR conglomerates

Today the biggest and best-known PR consultancies are owned by a small group of international marketing services or communications groups. These holding companies – which include direct marketing, digital and market research businesses – used to be dominated by advertising agencies. Although they still own most of the best-known advertising agencies, the leading role of advertising has been blunted by the increasing fragmentation of marketing methods, itself influenced by the fragmentation of the media.

Initially these groups were almost all American. The 1980s saw the emergence of UK-based groups, led by WPP's Sir Martin Sorrell, followed more recently by the emergence of the Australian-based Photon group and the Canadian-based Cossette group. How long will it be before Chinese or Indian groups become major players?

Many of the subsidiary companies listed in Table 5.1 were major players in their own country – or in some cases even internationally – before they were bought.

There are a number of business justifications given for the acquisition of a PR firm:

- the opportunity to cross-sell across marketing-related disciplines;
- the reduction of new business costs (at least in theory) as clients are able to buy a collection of services in one go;
- the benefit for group companies from economies of scale, with scope for sharing offices and so on;

**Table 5.1**

| The major listed marketing services groups and their main subsidiary companies | |
| --- | --- |
| Marketing group (in bold) and main PR subsidiaries | Home country |
| **WPP:** Burson-Marsteller, Cohn & Wolf, Finsbury, GCI Group, Hill & Knowlton, Ogilvy Worldwide, Shire Health (WPP also has a holding in UK quoted Chime plc.) | UK |
| **Omnicom:** Fishburn Hedges, Fleishman-Hillard, Gavin Anderson, Ketchum, Brodeur Worldwide, Porter Novelli, Clark & Weinstock, Blue Current, GPlus Europe, Staniforth Communications Pleon | US |
| **Huntsworth:** Citigate, EHPR, Grayling UK Ltd, Trimedia Harrison Cowley, Hasliman Taylor, The Red Consultancy, MMD | UK |
| **Chime:** Bell Pottinger Companies, Good Relations, Ozone, Resonate, Harvard, Insight Marketing, De facto, Baxter Hulme | UK |
| **IPG:** Golin Harris, Weber Shandwick, MWW Group | US |
| **Publicis:** MS&L, Freud Communications, Agence Pietri, Publicis Consultants | France |
| **Havas:** Euro RSCG, Maitland | France |
| **Cossette:** Band and Brown, Paine, Optimum | Canada |
| **Photon:** Frank, Hotwire, CPR | Australia |
| **FTI:** Financial Dynamics | US |
| **Next Fifteen:** Text 100, Bite Communications, Lexis PR (part share) | UK |

- the help major conglomerates can offer major clients in reaching international audiences while deploying a full range of marketing skills; and
- the large amount of money received by the owners, and the opportunity to play on a larger stage for the acquired companies and/or their escape from slow decline or even imminent disaster.

The regular purchase of PR firms is testimony to the indispensable role of PR within marketing services, while the retention by most conglomerates of a range of PR brand names – instead of attempting any crude rationalization – points to the perceived value of these well-established names. However it also indicates the ongoing problem that the groups have with what clients perceive as conflicts of interest. By maintaining several PR brand names it is easier to serve several competing clients under one roof.

Overall the amount of work shared within the conglomerates is limited. Clients often prefer to pick specialist services from different conglomerates, or from smaller suppliers outside the big groups. Internal rivalries among the big corporate purchasers of marketing services mean that people controlling different fiefdoms may want independent advice. Nor is the volume of international business as great as might have been hoped although it is undoubtedly growing as markets become more global: advertising may lend itself more readily to cross-border campaigns, but the subtleties of PR cannot be exported so readily. International PR campaigns seem to be one of those glamorous aspects of the business which the industry likes to dwell upon longingly, notwithstanding the patchiness of the business. Every year a spokesperson for one of the groups is sure to say; "This year integration and cross-border briefs are really taking off." But although there is growth the truth is less dramatic.

The US-based FTI consulting group who bought UK-based Financial Dynamics in September 2006 is very different from the other groups. This acquisition marked the first purchase of a PR firm by a non-marketing group and was seen by some as heralding a new era in which management consultancies would buy up communication firms. So far this is the only purchase of its type: the other big management and business consultancy groups have not followed suit. For now PR remains in the field of marketing rather than general management.

A kind of equilibrium may be being struck. PR firms will continue to emerge and grow, and to buy and be bought. The relatively fine profit margins which characterize PR (see p. 68) mean that it is hard for PR consultancies to achieve the levels of organic growth which satisfy external shareholders; buying another business can be a shortcut to showing better figures. It is certainly hard to detect any real strategic rationale in the proliferating company purchases within the PR industry beyond the desire for growth.[4] On the other hand the growth of the conglomerates is far from inexorable. Wall Street and the City are not overenthusiastic about media businesses, which not only operate on fine margins, but are also notoriously vulnerable both to economic cycles and to the fact that their greatest assets, senior, experienced people, can walk out at any time. Big firms may wish to operate like cherished upmarket department stores but can come perilously close to behaving like "stack 'em high" supermarkets, leaving the way open for smaller specialist consultancies, which continue to sprout and which are often formed by dissatisfied staff who have quit the big firms.

Indeed, according to the International Communications Consultancy Organization, internationally independence remains the dominant model.[5] With the exception of Greece, the Czech Republic, and Russia, most consultancy trade associations have a membership that is independent rather than part of a group. This of course may reflect the large number of small agencies in any country, plus the reluctance of some of the big firms to join trade associations that they believe are better at helping small firms.

## The persistence of "penny packet" PR

Statistics and anecdotal evidence suggest that the great majority of the myriad of PR agencies employ at most a handful of people, operating within informal networks where extra assistance can be hired as required. They service a handful of clients. The fortunate few may scale the heights of the industry, sometimes very quickly, perhaps undertaking some acquisitions or undergoing some mergers along the way (see the boxed case histories of Hill & Knowlton and GCI). Overall the center of gravity of the PR consultancy sector as defined by staff numbers is a level or two higher than a cottage industry – consultancies with more than a handful of staff but not many more. In the United Kingdom's *PR Week* 2007 Consultancy League tables the average number of employees in the firms ranked 50–150 was 26 (although this figure seems somewhat high as in some cases there is a 50% variation in staffing levels for the same fee income).[6] The figures for the US *PR Week* tables are broadly similar. And of course there are many hundreds if not thousands of much smaller firms.

Whatever the precise figure, these averages reveal an industry characterized by a very low level of concentration. Few PR consultancies in the leading US and UK markets have employed more than a small proportion of the overall numbers employed in PR. For example in 2007 Bell Pottinger (comprising around 16 businesses), the biggest UK PR group according to *PR Week*, employed 418 staff, a fraction under 1% of the total number of people estimated by the CIPR to be employed in PR in the United Kingdom. The United States shows a similar pattern. Edelman, which tops the O'Dwyer list, had 2,259 employees in 2006 in the United States, around 1% of all those estimated to work in PR in the country according to the Department of Labor.[7]

Critics of the PR industry focus on big consultancies, but PR has never been dominated by big firms to the same extent as the legal or accountancy professions – nor have the upper echelons of the industry been as congealed. New entrants constantly emerge. This partly reflects the ease with which new PR firms can be set up, but also the willingness of clients to hire such firms provided the personalities are right – and as we have mentioned senior talent is forever jumping ship. It may also reflect the difficulty of sustaining creative talent and energy within the bureaucratic behemoths that large firms can become.

The same is true for turnover: if the industry's fees are measured in billions of dollars or pounds then the biggest players only account for a small proportion of this. The point is important, as many approach the PR industry as though it were akin to the media industries with their much higher levels of concentration. When someone in PR talks about the consultancy industry they are usually talking about their small bit of it. This has an impact on discussions about the PR industry, particularly as many prominent spokespeople for the industry represent their own small firms rather than the major international players. In the absence of solid research PR people – however distinguished or well-connected – offer views and information based on their experience and what they can glean from friends and colleagues. As a result they can usually only examine one or two square centimeters of the PR painting. Even the consultancy trade bodies only represent a minority of businesses operating in the industry. Writers for the trade press, such as *PR Week*, are among the few who have a clear overview of the industry.

### Are PR firms profitable?

Edelman, the largest agency in the United States, achieves revenue per employee of $144,000,[8] whilst its UK equivalent, Bell Pottinger, achieves £112,000 per employee.[9] In the United Kingdom, outside the top 10 consultancies, fee levels of around £70–90,000 per staff member are typical. In the United States the figures for firms ranked 10 to 40 range from a very modest $110,000 to an impressive $377,000. In general fee levels are much higher for financial PR firms which, particularly when involved in mergers and acquisitions, can have an immediate effect on share

price and in turn on the personal wealth of the client's board of directors. As David Rigg, a senior PR practitioner in the United Kingdom,
once told one of the authors, "If a consultant can find out what keeps
the Chief Executive awake at night he can make a fortune."

PR firms extract a typical pretax profit margin of around 13.7%
on their business according to a UK study by Willott Kingston Smith
(WKS), an accountancy practice which specializes in providing
financial and management advice to creative, communications, and
consultancy businesses.[10] Although this is better than creative communication disciplines such as design and advertising – which struggle to achieve margins of 10% – it is well below the margins of around
20% achieved by the less creative but more numerate media buying
agencies, and much less than some management and software
consultancies.

An examination of WKS reports over the last decade shows how
quickly this can change for the worse. One of the paradoxes of PR
and related marketing services is that spending falls sharply with
first signs of an economic downturn. It might seem logical that
spending on projecting one's organization and what it does should,
if anything, increase in times of difficulty, but the evidence points
the other way. Proponents of PR as a vital management discipline
have always had problems with the way in which it is often treated
as a dispensable luxury.

The truth is that PR, in common with other "creative" businesses,
is not particularly profitable. We can only make intelligent guesses
as to why this should be. The most obvious reason would seem to be
that people start PR consultancies because they are good at PR and
want to be their own boss. Making money is, at least initially, a
secondary motive. PR practitioners are also creative and imagina-
tive, or at least that is what they like to think. This might make them
entertaining companions, but it does not necessarily make them
millionaires. Another possible reason is that the industry is not big
enough in terms of its total value or concentration for a sophisticated
management class to evolve. In a crowded and competitive market
there is always someone hungry or desperate enough to undercut
others. Given that measurement is difficult and real value hard to
prove, a lower price can be tempting to a client uncertain of the worth
of PR. When PR people lament the fact that their fees fall short of
those of professional services firms in fields such as law and accountancy, they forget that such long-established professions have their

own well-placed advocates at the summit of most businesses in the form of financial directors and company secretaries. They also offer services which businesses are compelled to use and which are demonstrably of "life-or-death" significance.

As far back as 2003 WKS identified a lessening in the dominance of advertising as a discrete discipline, and noted that marketing communication groups which were still acquisitive tended to buy "below-the-line" marketing services businesses such as public relations. This trend has continued. Stock markets may not like people-dependent creative businesses, but they do at least prefer those such as WPP that have PR as a significant part of their business.

### Hill & Knowlton[11]

Hill & Knowlton would be the epitome of a large US public relations firm, but for the fact that it is now owned by the British WPP group. Its origins go back to the early days of PR, and it was the first of the major US firms to develop a large international network. While rankings change from time to time, Hill & Knowlton has often featured in league tables as the largest PR consultancy in the world.

The company's founder was John W. Hill, who set up a "corporate publicity office" in 1927 in Cleveland, Ohio. He was already 37 and had formerly worked as a journalist, but had also dabbled in publicity work, creating a newsletter for a company which became one of his new business's first clients. Others included Otis Steel, United Alloy Steel, Standard Oil of Ohio, and Republic Steel.

During the Depression Hill took into partnership the public relations director of a failing client, Donald Knowlton. In 1934 Hill moved his headquarters to New York, in order to serve as public relations counsel to the American Iron and Steel Institute. Knowlton remained in Ohio and ceased to be involved with the company's development.

Hill & Knowlton experienced steady growth within the United States. Although originally dependent on the steel industry, in the post-Second World War era the firm worked for aircraft manufacturers and became instrumental in cultivating the idea that air power was the solution to America's strategic problems. In the 1950s Hill & Knowlton was also the firm the tobacco industry turned to as it faced the first evidence of the link between smoking and cancer. Hill & Knowlton recommended the establishment of the Tobacco Industry Research Council which undertook research of its own in an attempt to cast doubt on the health fears.

Hill & Knowlton was an important industry pioneer in other respects. During the 1950s Hill & Knowlton led the way in setting up international offices, following US business overseas. Today its London office also serves as the headquarters of the firm's Europe, Middle East, and Africa network, with 27 offices.

Hill & Knowlton worked with schools and teachers on behalf of its steel industry client and set up an Environmental Health Unit from 1966, while John Hill emphasized the importance of community relations as early as 1963. It also blazed a trail with innovative business methods, developing a system of standard fees and staff-time charges to replace its haphazard methods in the 1940s. It borrowed from advertising the idea of testing copy in the 1950s, and used computers from the 1960s.

Hill managed the firm until 1962 and remained active within it until his death in 1977. In 1980 Hill & Knowlton was acquired by the JWT advertising group, which was in turn acquired by WPP in 1987. Hill & Knowlton's historian, Karen Miller, explains how, under pressure to demonstrate improved financial results, both growth and income, the company's new chief executive, Robert Dilenschneider, engaged in self-promotion, which included publishing a book, *Power and Influence: Mastering the Art of Persuasion*.[12] Clients were accepted on a project basis – not just for the long-term counsel upon which Hill had insisted. The agency's policy of refusing political and religious accounts was also discarded, and the Church of Scientology was taken on as a client (leading to the loss of Hill & Knowlton's important Smithkline Beecham account).

Following Iraq's invasion of Kuwait in 1990 Hill & Knowlton undertook probably its biggest project of all time, when it assisted the Kuwaiti Government in exile in its bid to persuade world – and particularly American opinion – to back the liberation of their country. This included the notorious and apparently untrue allegations about Iraqi soldiers plucking Kuwaiti babies from incubators and leaving them to die, although it must be said that the story was swallowed whole by the credulous media.

Although the account was high-profile and lucrative it marked a watershed in Hill & Knowlton's history. In 1991 Dilenscheider left, as did his successor the following year. The Hill & Knowlton star was descending. The agency undertook research to find out what was going wrong and found that potential clients were put off by the way its large size seemed to denote high costs, insensitivity, and slow responses. The reforms included a move toward greater specialization including, for example, marketing communications groups for gay and lesbian audiences.

Today a much revived Hill & Knowlton is still owned by the WPP group, which owns 4 other major PR groups, and is estimated to be one of the top 5 PR firms in the world with over 2000 staff, and 72 offices in 41 countries. Its size and success attracts criticism from the likes of Corporate Watch and hyperbole from the likes of Wikipedia[13] which said of the company: "Its reach and control over mass media allows the firm to have direct impact on world events, public policy and shaping news stories."

**GCI UK to Europe** by Adrian Wheeler, former Chairman of GCI Europe

Sterling PR, which became GCI in 1990, was typical of a dozen or so public relations companies which started up in the United Kingdom in the seventies and were lucky enough to be in the right place, doing the right thing, at the right time. In 1970 the UK PR consultancy business was embryonic, earning £20 million a year. It grew rapidly during the eighties and nineties – pausing for recessions – and is now estimated to be worth over £1 billion.

Sterling was set up in 1976 by two partners who shared three clients, two employees, and two rooms in a central London mansion block. It was born on the damp November day when the owner of the consultancy where John Brill and I both worked called us into his office and announced his intention of retiring. To our astonishment, he meant there and then. We decided to call it "Sterling" because we wanted our future employees to feel it was their company as much as ours; this principle did not, however, apply to the equity.

Our first step was to buy two tickets to New York on our American Express cards. We had the idea that US companies would want professional PR help when they were expanding into Europe via London. We thought this was an original insight. The trip paid off. We returned with our fourth client – The Federation of American-Controlled Shipping – and frequent visits to see them gave us the chance to build a substantial book of US business over the next five years.

I would like to say that we had a grand plan for the company, but we didn't. We just loved the PR business; there were no rules, everyone was making it up as they went along, and we were having much more fun than anyone else except The Rolling Stones. The best thing was that PR was producing terrific results. Clients were excited and told their friends. To us, it didn't seem like work; we often carried on right through the night. That seemed like fun, too.

On our tenth birthday in 1986 we took stock. Sterling had 30 staff, £3m in revenue and a top-flight client list: Philips – who paid us a million a year; the Jamaica Tourist Board; Food & Wine from France; Richard Ellis; Stewart Wrightson, at that time the largest insurance-broker in the United Kingdom; chemical giants ICI and Ciba-Geigy; and fourteen others. Our competitors – Shandwick, Paragon, Countrywide, QBO, and the US agencies – were well financed, while Sterling was still run with an overdraft secured on my house and John's house. We considered acquiring, merging, and selling. During the year, we held meetings with 60 potential acquirees, merger-partners, and acquirers.

We chose Grey Communications Group for three reasons. They knew nothing about PR, so we would remain autonomous. They believed in "singularity of brand," so we would be the only Grey Group PR firm. They also offered us the best price for our shares. With Grey's backing we were able to grow twice as quickly. During the nineties, we continued putting on 10–15% a year organically, but we could now make acquisitions. Our first was MacAvoy Bailey, a City and public affairs consultancy. My partner, John, left the firm shortly after our earn-out finished in 1990, as did Claire Walker – to found Firefly.

In 1995 we started GCI Healthcare as a parallel brand, and in the same year began negotiating with Rupert Ashe, the owner of Focus Communications – our City affiliate – to acquire his company. Before 2000 we had acquired Lay & Partners, sports sponsorship specialists; Jane Howard Public Relations, a retail and FMCG (fast moving consumer goods) boutique; Maureen Cropper Communications, who specialized in OTC (over the counter) healthcare; and Delaney Communications, who concentrated on retail financial services. In 2001 GCI UK was the seventh-largest PR firm in the United Kingdom.

In 1994 Grey decided to extend the GCI brand in Europe, and GCI UK was closely involved in making acquisitions and opening offices as fast as we could go.

In 2004 Grey was bought by Sir Martin Sorrell's WPP group, a move which saw GCI join the WPP stable of major international PR groups. Today GCI have offices or affiliates in most parts of the world.

Public relations has no barriers to entry. Anyone with the wit, a bit of experience, and the nerve can set up their own consultancy. Every year, many do just this; one in three stays the course and one in five does well enough to mount a serious challenge to the larger firms, like GCI. There are few other business service sectors where clients can choose between so many suppliers, large and small, or where the competitive landscape changes so continuously. This is good for clients, and good for PR.

In many ways, GCI's story exemplifies the history of the PR consultancy business.

### Specialist PR

The most basic specialist division in public relations is between corporate and consumer PR. The former concerns itself with a company's reputation and its relationship with stakeholders, while the latter is about supporting marketing objectives. Most of the big PR firms still divide themselves in this way. However, PR's tendency to specialize does not stop but begins at this point.

One of the characteristics that distinguishes PR from other marketing disciplines is this propensity to specialize. The advertising agency business does not have a plethora of specialist shops covering everything from healthcare, personal finance, and technology through to fashion, food, travel, and restaurants. Most advertising agencies claim to cover most, if not all, of these business sectors under one roof – with the possible exception of healthcare, a sector in which communication is highly regulated. Not so PR.

Each of these sectors – and there are many more – is served by a number of (usually small) specialist PR firms. And even the big generalist agencies have specialist divisions covering many of these sectors. There are also skill, as opposed to sector, based PR specialists ranging from lobbying and financial PR through to crisis management and internal communications.

### Sector specialists

The rationale for some sector specialists is the need for technical and/or regulatory knowledge. Obvious examples of this are healthcare and, certainly until recently, technology PR. The former often involves communicating with specialist audiences such as doctors, and is highly regulated: in the United Kingdom, for example, prescription drugs cannot be directly promoted to the public. In the case of information technology, as personal computers have become mainstream the need to understand and then translate the jargon has declined. Most mainstream PR people can now do high tech PR work and indeed are perhaps better at speaking to general audiences than "wirehead" PRs. Moreover, the specialist computer press has shrunk. In consequence a lot of former high tech PR consultancies are now trying to reposition themselves.

The techniques specialists use are similar to those of mainstream PR with a heavy, although not exclusive, emphasis on media relations. Unlike generalists they quite often have direct experience in the sector they are serving, are able to talk the clients "jargon," and will be familiar with regulatory issues. While some healthcare and high tech specialist consultancies have grown to a reasonable size many of the other sector specialists such as travel, food, and fashion have remained small.

This is for three interrelated reasons. First, these sectors are in themselves characterized by a large number of small businesses which cannot afford an effective in-house PR function or to hire larger mainstream consultancies. (Small businesses naturally tend to employ small consultancies, and indeed large consultancies would often be disdainful about small accounts.) Second, specialist firms also seem to emerge when a sector has a range of its own specialist media, including magazines, newspaper sections, or programs on national and regional media (often funded by related advertising), and dedicated journalists. Third, these sectors are often characterized by strong personalities – fashion designers, chefs, artists, and cultural and social figures of many kinds. This is distinct from the blander corporate personae of most big companies, and lends itself to smaller scale, more personal PR, often by PR's own personalities.

Fashion and travel, for example, apart from being perceived as glamorous, generate high levels of dedicated media and media coverage. This in turn justifies specialist consultancies and practitioners. Indeed the relationship between the PRs and the journalists in these sorts of sectors means that there is a high level of movement, usually from journalism to PR, due to higher PR salaries.

Personal financial services PR (as opposed to financial PR related to mergers and acquisitions and share prices), though it operates in a highly regulated market, has not spawned many specialist firms. As with high tech PR this is partly because financial services have become more mainstream. The other factor here seems to be that most financial service firms are large enough to employ in-house PR people, only using consultancies for brand building or to cope with peaks in workload. Similarly the automotive industry, despite its size and importance, has generated few specialist PR shops. Indeed major industries such as the utilities, transport, and communications, despite their size and wealth, have little in the way of dedicated media and consequently few specialist PR firms serving them.

So the factors underpinning sector specialization would seem to be one or more of the following:

1. heavy regulation;
2. technical complexity;
3. dedicated sector media;
4. the dominance of individual personalities; and
5. medium to small-sized client businesses.

The reasons that PR is able to service this ever-changing range of demands are twofold: the cost of setting up a PR firm is so low; and, second, because, in a business sector which is based on personalities rather than professional qualifications, clients can easily follow their favorite PR person as they move around from mega consultancy to start-up firm – or even offer them an in-house position.

### Skill specialists

Skill specialist PR firms do not service industry sectors but seek to meet generic industry needs. For example lobbyists specialize in understanding and influencing the political and regulatory process on behalf of their clients (see p. 145). Similarly financial or City PR firms (in the United Kingdom) or Investor Relations firms (in the United States) specialize in understanding the capital and equity markets. And yet, while both operate in areas that are to some degree regulated, the regulation is neither so complex nor so technical that an intelligent generalist PR person could not grasp it. It is knowledge and experience of another kind, of gossip and "politicking" rather than simply reading the press on a daily basis, which is needed to manage and play the political process or the equity markets. The expertise of such specialists represents less a laboriously studied body of knowledge than an interest, coupled with cumulatively acquired experience of their area. It also takes a certain attitude. It is no accident that a large percentage of lobbyists have political ambitions. Lobbying also makes a nice home for politicians who have been rejected by the voters.

The gossipy knowledge that investor relations specialists and lobbyists have is important as their clients will often be new to, or at least inexperienced, in the fields they cover. As Irwin Ross put it, the art of name-dropping

> is a serious business tactic, designed to impress present and future clients with the PR man's easy familiarity with the potentates of industry and government. But name-dropping alone is not enough; the accomplished inside dopester must be in a position to pass along scraps of information which are not yet in the public domain.[14]

It is difficult to hire high quality people to work in-house to play these advisory roles. Flotations, mergers, acquisitions, and lobbying for legislative change are not for most businesses everyday events or continuous processes – unlike marketing – but they are of critical

importance. So it is that financial PRs, closely followed by lobbyists, tend to be better paid than their generalist siblings. According
to UK-based Median Recruitment, in 2006 the average salary for an
account director in a financial PR consultancy was between £40,000
and £80,000+. In contrast the equivalent salary for an account director
in consumer PR was only £38,000 to £55,000.[15]

There are also other similarities with sector specialists: the worlds
of high finance and politics have their own specialist media and journalists; the cost of entry for new specialist firms is low; and the importance of personalities is high – as is the case for fashion, food, and
travel.

Employee or internal communication specialists are another group
of skill – or audience – specialists, although a surprisingly small
group given the potential size of the employee audience. There are
several reasons for this specialism's comparatively small size and
low visibility.

First, most employee communications work (see Chapter 10) is conducted in-house. It therefore attracts less attention than areas of PR
that are well served by consultancies which have to spend a lot of
time promoting their wares and the benefits of what they do. Second,
employee communications – be it in-house or consultancy-sourced –
often comes under the control of the human resources or personnel
department. This means that it can fall outside the boundaries of
public relations and not be described as PR. It also has little involvement with PR's heartland of media relations and is thus seldom seen
or heard of, beyond its tightly defined target audiences. Finally
employee communications is less labor intensive than PR directed at
external audiences. Employers create and control their own media, be
they newsletters, web-casts or business TV. Internal communicators
have no need to spend time researching, cajoling, flattering, and helping cynical or even antagonistic journalists. As we argue later on,
employee or internal communications is one of the purest forms of
propaganda.

In addition, there is the much talked about specialist area of
digital PR. Most senior PR practitioners and commentators say that
digital PR – by which they mean everything from interactive websites, to blogging, social networks, and online news – should be
central to and integrated in every PR campaign. We broadly agree
with this, while noting that there are large groups in society and

large parts of the population of the world for whom the digital world is a distant dream.

In response to the rise of the internet, most large PR agencies have set up digital practices and many small specialist consultancies have emerged – though presumably these will be dissolved or disappear as digital integration into the mainstream becomes a reality. Certainly the need to influence and persuade audiences through third parties such as bloggers and online journalists fits our definition of public relations (see p. 102). Digital PR, like Corporate Social Responsibility, also gives agencies something new and exciting to sell to clients.

However, PR does not have the digital space all to itself. Many other marketing disciplines – not least advertising – are also jumping on the digital bandwagon and may be seen as more credible than PR when it comes to data analysis and the number crunching aspects of the digital world.

## In-house PR and the eunuchs of modern corporate life

Despite its high profile it is estimated by the CIPR[16] that in the United Kingdom the consultancy sector only accounts for around 18% of all PR people. The remaining 82% work in-house, directly employed by the organizations they serve. In-house PR departments – often lurking under the guise of "corporate communications" or "communications" or other titles – are now ubiquitous in all but the smallest organizations, throughout the private, public, and voluntary sectors. Even in the United States, birthplace of modern PR, senior figures in the consultancy sector can recall working with sizeable companies that lacked any PR capability of their own, and relied on PR consultancies for all aspects of their public relations. This is now rare. Organizations which once outsourced their entire PR realize that routine work can be achieved more cost-effectively in-house: a consultancy after all aims to recover much more than its consultants' salaries when it hires them out, as it seeks to cover overheads and achieve a margin for its shareholders. As in-house PR has grown it has also achieved the critical mass required to undertake more complex PR tasks on its own, and organizations using in-house PR enjoy the advantage of readier physical access.

Just as the job-titles of in-house PR practitioners vary, so do the size and role of their departments. It is harder to generalize about the in-house sector than the world of PR consultancy because the former is even more atomized – few organizations employ as many communications or PR professionals directly as the big PR consultancies. Thus, despite more PR people working in-house than in the consultancy sector, they are in even less of a position to have an overview of in-house PR, let alone public relations in general.

In-house PR is afflicted by a paradox. While most business leaders concede that PR is important, no-one has been able to quantify its importance convincingly – and certainly not to demonstrate its financial value (although attempts have been, and continue to be, made – see pp. 161–171). As a result there is no real business rationale for determining the size of in-house PR departments or their budgets. Instead these tend to be the product of informal processes that are heavily dependent on the ambition and personal influence of senior PR people. Past experience may be taken into account, alongside the size of rival organizations' PR departments – or the PR budget may be based on a percentage of the organization's overall spending on marketing communications.

The inability of in-house PR departments to justify their existence with robust financial figures does not necessarily mean that they, or the people who run them, lack power. Typically a large in-house PR team will include a communications or corporate affairs director. They play the role of courtiers: seldom on the main board of the company, they enjoy extensive access to their chief executives – to whom they typically report – as well as exclusive control of media relations. Their real influence hinges on their relationship with the CEO – and other key figures in the organization – and the extent to which their advice is respected.[17] Other senior figures in the company may run large departments, control massive budgets, and have their own power bases, but senior in-house PR people are essentially creatures of the CEO, with whom they often stand or fall. Unlike other members of the senior management team they are most unlikely ever to become CEOs themselves, and so do not pose a direct threat to the status quo. They can be compared to palace eunuchs: well-placed, well-informed confidants who play a vital role behind the scenes without challenging the organization's succession strategy.

It is arguable that as CEOs confront an ever more complex business environment – particularly the real or potential challenges of regulation – adept in-house PR chiefs will grow in importance. Overall the balance of power has shifted in favor of in-house PR: both the numbers and the quality of the personnel have improved. Indeed many in-house practitioners have consultancy backgrounds. A move in-house can be seen as a good career move for senior consultancy staff that are put off by the managerialism of big consultancies and are not in the fortunate position of having their own businesses to sell.

Nonetheless turf wars between corporate affairs directors and marketing directors are common. Their relative power will depend on the nature of the business, their personalities, and their degree of access to the rest of the senior management team. In the past much of a marketing director's power derived from the fact that they "owned" the advertising budget (a sum that did – and still does for some organizations – run into many millions of dollars/pounds). In budgetary terms the corporate affairs director was the poor relation. However the fragmentation of media spend and the rise in the importance of public relations has led to a gradual shift in the center of gravity toward PR, though tensions between the two persist. Some – though not many – businesses have overcome this problem by combining the two roles.

**Anne Groves, Global Head of Public Relations at the leading international law firm Clifford Chance**

Anne Groves coordinates a global PR network for Clifford Chance which is made up as follows:

London – 4 people (including herself)

Frankfurt – 3
USA – 2
Milan – 2
Paris – 2
Amsterdam – 2
Brussels – 1
Budapest – 1
Moscow – 1
Madrid – 1
Hong Kong – 2

The total PR team comprises 17 women and four men. Most are in their thirties, although six are in their forties or older. Of the four in the UK, all are women. The team has degrees in Politics and English from Kingston University, English and History from Auckland University, NZ, and Marketing from the University of Central England. Anne has a degree in English from London University.

**A day in her life**

| | |
|---|---|
| 7.00 a.m. | Check email; read faxes of Clifford Chance national newspaper coverage at home. |
| 8.00 a.m. | On way in pick up emails, mostly from New York office (and anyone else who has emailed overnight) on my beloved "blackberry"; read work papers (position papers on current issues, drafts of documents). |
| 9.00 a.m. | Arrive in office. Scan online news service of all coverage of CC and our main competitors, scan newspapers to check who's writing what in our sector, and current topical issues. PR team passes on coverage to spokespeople concerned and to internal communications team for possible inclusion in daily electronic internal newsletter. Note anything significant to add to our weekly "media news" update internally. |
| 9.30 a.m. | Call Hong Kong office for regular catch-up on plans and issues with our head of communications there |
| 10.15 a.m. | Start drafting a briefing note for our managing partner for a forthcoming journalist meeting (background on the journalist, recent examples of stories they've written, notes on what we want to talk about, and what may come up) |
| | Take/return calls from an FT journalist writing a piece about opportunities for young professionals in countries which have just joined the EU; from the London correspondent of the *New York Times* on an M&A story; and from our media coverage evaluation agency on the next quarterly report on our media coverage compared to our main |

competitors. Ring a newswire journalist contact to suggest that we set up a meeting for them with some spokespeople at CC who have some views on their specialist area

11.00 a.m.     Meeting with one of our competition lawyers on forthcoming competition issues in the EU. These include a Competition Commission enquiry on store cards, a planned joint client seminar with the Office of Fair Trading, and further opportunities for comment on the EU Commission's enquiry into Microsoft.

12.00 p.m.     Write up notes from the meeting – add to the PR's team's "quarterly plan" which identifies opportunities we should follow up

1.00 p.m.      Lunch with the business features editor of *The Times* – one of my favorite contacts.

3.00 p.m.      Regular monthly meeting with the in-house PR team and our PR agency to plan the next initiatives, discuss issues etc.

4.30 p.m.      Return calls from a business magazine doing a piece on trends in private equity deals; from a legal trade paper researching a piece on global expansion in law firms – and pass on request, with advice, to relevant partners on how we can best respond.

5.00 p.m.      Catch up with plans for a forthcoming hospitality event aimed at the firm's main senior contacts

5.45 p.m.      Fix time for regular global PR group conference call and distribute draft agenda. Continue briefing note for the managing partner

6.00 p.m.      Call our head of communications in the Americas to discuss progress on projects and forthcoming issues. These include opportunities for promoting the New York practice in the *Wall Street Journal* (we have close relations with the *Wall Street Journal* London too, and keep each other updated on PR activity for all media outlets where we have active relationships in different countries), the possibility of a partner in Washington DC joining the legal team at a client company, and the updating of the briefing note document we provide for the senior management spokespeople – plus general gossip. (I have a similar regular conversation with our head of communications in Hong Kong as well.)

6.45 p.m.     Finish briefing document for managing partner and talk through the forthcoming meeting with him.

7.15 p.m.     Finish off emails

7.30 p.m.     Leave office; read minutes of meetings, relevant newspaper and magazine articles on way home

In the past the corporate PR practitioner – be it in-house or consultancy – would nearly always answer to the head of corporate communications while their consumer counterpart would answer to the vice president or director of marketing. Although this practice still persists there has been a recent trend to take a more holistic or "joined-up" view of communications, reflecting the need to integrate lobbying and corporate social responsibility into mainstream marketing programs.

One problem with this is that the pursuit of profit does not always sit comfortably with the quest for an excellent reputation. The marketing department may want to increase sales of an alcoholic beverage popular with young people, while the PR people want to convince regulators and lobbyists that their organization has a social conscience and fosters responsible drinking. It can be difficult to satisfy the media's – and consumers' – contradictory demands for easy availability, low prices and saintly social behavior. Not surprisingly PR people sometimes tie themselves in knots and can appear disingenuous as they try to do so.

Other areas of conflict include employee communications, which human resources departments like to hold on to; and financial PR, which some financial directors think they need to control. This is a circular argument. Communication is so important you need a specialist to do it, and financial relations and employee relations are

**Figure 5.1**
**A simplified diagram of a large in-house "public relations" department**

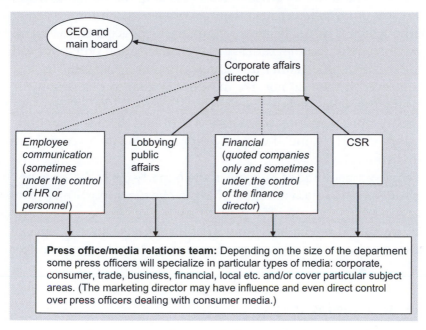

so important that you need a specialist to do them too. Ultimately where the specialist sits is an issue only of interest to those playing corporate musical chairs!

Why then do PR consultancies continue to exist? What can they deliver or achieve more cost-effectively than their in-house counterparts?

First, an external consultancy can bring a freshness of perspective which an in-house team cannot, caught up as it is in the web of office politics and corporate culture which characterize any organization. Consultancies can be more objective and, it is claimed, are better able to understand the world as the client's intended target audiences see it. It is no accident that PR consultancies are increasingly brought in to create and run high-profile one-off campaigns, leaving more run-of-the-mill reactive media relations work to in-house teams. Freshness of approach does not mean absence of knowledge: by definition an external consultancy can have a range of up-to-the-minute experience derived from working for related business areas, and even competitors, in a way that an in-house team cannot.

A consultancy can also leverage its client base: if it is working for two or more organizations which are not in competition and yet have some crossover points in the popular imagination it is ideally placed to undertake mutually advantageous PR activity. Big players in the PR consultancy field can also acquire contacts and influence over the media which it would be hard for any in-house team to rival. This is true of some of the biggest financial firms. At the other end of the scale it is true of celebrity and entertainment PR firms. The media know, even if they do not like to admit it, that to please some top-ranking financial consultancies such as Brunswick opens the door to more tip-offs and exclusives, whereas to offend them is potentially to be starved of the same. If you only represent one firm you only have one card to play.

Finally, consultancies can contribute expertise which it may not be cost-effective to retain in-house: this may be the opportunity to meet and consult a particular PR guru; to enable an overseas company to acquire a local media handling capability; to use specific specialist skills; or simply provide extra pairs of hands to meet occasional needs.

## The tail of the industry

As the different branches of the PR industry have grown in scale a range of small "component industries" have come to shelter under their shade. Often these were activities which the emerging PR consultancies originally undertook themselves on behalf of clients, and for which they charged handsomely. But as business volumes swelled entrepreneurial individuals spotted the potential to establish independent niche operations. PR consultancies' loss of these ancillary sources of income had the paradoxical effect that as the industry started to talk more and more about a world beyond media relations, an ever greater proportion of its income came from exactly that.

These services are advertised in many PR directories and websites. Another source of information is the main international trade paper, *PR Week*. The overall scale of these support services is not great, but the outsourcing of such work is growing. We have drawn the examples below from *PR Week*'s UK edition, November 23, 2007 (pp. 32–36).

At least one of the services predates the PR industry. *Press cutting firms* which supply clippings on any topic (this now includes the provision of recordings and transcripts) can be traced back to the nineteenth century. PR people in all sectors make extensive use of such services.

Other services underline PR's focus on media relations. The chief categories are *media distribution* (the distribution of press releases and other materials to the media); *media monitoring and evaluation*; and *media and interview training* (which PR people routinely arrange for their clients or employers). There are also self-explanatory services such as "prize management," "celebrity services," "speakers and personalities" and "web-based PR software." Others are designed to assist with *media production* for PR people's own or managed media – the newsletters, DVDs, websites, and so forth which they generate themselves as part of their work. Services which can be used across the PR spectrum include photography, translation, and writing and editorial work. Edward Bernays – nephew twice over of Sigmund Freud and godfather of modern PR – would be interested to see that someone is offering themselves as a specialist PR psychologist.

These services are contracted out because it is more cost-effective. Few firms can afford to retain such in-house services or data-based functions when specialist suppliers can achieve unmatchable economies of scale.

More surprising is the announcement by one company, Text 100, that it is contracting out functions previously seen as core consultancy tasks. As announced in *PR Week*, this includes writing basic press releases, putting together case studies, and general account administration and secondary research tasks.[18] The service is called "Global Resource Optimization" and, according to Text's regional director, this allows clients to "tap into round the clock services and gives then the opportunity to lower the cost of performing time-intensive tasks."

The new service is being run from Text's existing office in Mumbai, India. The hope is that the money saved will be spent on higher margin, more strategic, services. The arguments against the innovation are that it will be difficult to maintain quality control and that PR involves "nuances" that require specific, local cultural knowledge that someone thousands of miles away cannot have. It raises a further specter. With news agencies such as Reuters outsourcing journalism to India,[19] in theory both the raw material and the finished product for domestic news stories in Europe or North America could become the handiwork of Indian suppliers: true globalization of the information marketplace.

But if the Text model succeeds it could transform the PR industry. Fewer of the young graduate worker bees so beloved of the consultancy world will be needed. Margins will improve, enabling consultancies to hire better staff and invest more in their training. PR consultancy will be more about advice than execution – more like real consultancy. But over this hovers a huge question mark. How much real demand is there for high level strategic advice? Doesn't the industry already offer this? It says it does. At what point does strategic advice become management consultancy – a form of consultancy that tends to rely on numbers and systems, neither of which plays to the PR industry's strengths? The danger must be that Text will save money for its clients without making any extra money for itself.

# CHAPTER 6

# The people in PR

## Exuberant, persuasive dilettantes?

So what kind of people work in PR? Why do they do it and what do they earn? And where do they come from?

PR people come from all walks of life. Some have degrees, some do not. Some are old hands tired of the corporate grind, others are natural entrepreneurs, and some are just passing through as they seek a career Holy Grail. What unites them is not so much demographics as personality. Jackall and Hirota offer a well-judged list of the seven characteristics of a successful practitioner:

1. The knack of entertaining clients with clever casual conversation
2. Graceful acceptance of being the focus of attention
3. A talent for thinking on one's feet
4. Willingness to star at client presentations
5. An ability to mystify the "creative leap"
6. Knowing when to switch to rational discourse
7. Enthusiasm[1]

Not every PR person will fit this bill, but it is noticeable how many tick at least some of the boxes, and how many consultancy heads tick nearly all the boxes. It is also notable how few other industries require this mix of abilities.

### PR dilettantes

Another characteristic needed in PR is a broad set of interests, perhaps to the exclusion of a deep interest in any one thing. Trevor Morris – one of the authors of this book – was described by his first boss as an "intelligent dilettante." It was not entirely meant as a compliment.

However, the expression, given a more positive twist, aptly describes a number of successful PR players. Given the premium placed on expert and in-depth knowledge this is counterintuitive and hard for some PR people to admit – but it captures an important truth.

> It is often said that one of the great ironies of PR – which claims to be about the management of reputation – is its failure to explain and justify its own role to the public. One reason for this may be that this is one arena in which PR people cease to be dilettantes: immersed in their own subject and the obscurities of its language they fail to make a comprehensible and convincing case for what they do.

One of the things that people often get wrong when hiring PR advice is to say they "want someone who really understands our business." What they actually want is someone who understands their business just a bit better than the people with whom they need to communicate. A good consultant should be able to tell their client how the world sees them, and then be able to communicate back to the world in a way that is relevant and engaging. This is hard to achieve if you have become as mired in the intricacies of widget production as the client. Even in-house PR people have roving briefs – they deal with whatever is to the fore in their organization, which by definition will keep changing. If being a dilettante means possessing a superficial knowledge of a lot of things then PR people should be happy to wear that crown.

The experts on the complexities and the detail will work elsewhere in the organization and are often people with specialist training and experience. PR's role is to act as an intermediary between an organization's specialist staff – who are seldom able adequately to explain what they do to those who lack their expertise – and their intended audiences, who need information and messages to which they as nonspecialists can relate. In the relatively rare cases where specialists are good at explaining their area of expertise to wider audiences they are often themselves drawn in to PR or part-PR roles.

It also seems to be the case that PR consultants work best in comparatively small units. Peter Hehir, a senior industry figure (see p. 54), once told one of the authors that he thought the optimum size for a self-contained PR firm was around 100 people. The figure might be arbitrary but was based on the contention that good PR people tend to be sociable and need a sense of belonging if they are to be creative and work to their utmost. As we have seen, very few firms have more than a 100 staff working from one site, and even those that do break their staff down into smallish, mainly self-contained, teams. Nonetheless the most common criticism made of big PR firms is that they lack creativity.

As might be expected of an industry largely and increasingly made up of young, city-dwelling, university-educated women, PR consultants tend to be sociable, liberal, and generally optimistic about life. PR people like to be liked. This is in contrast to PR people's nemesis: the journalist. In our experience they are more likely to be cynical about people's motives; pessimistic about the future; and prefer working on their own to working in a team. These are probably just the sort of virtues needed to ensure a free and critical press!

**A day in the life of Jessica Bush, PR Director at top London health and beauty PR specialist Kilpatrick PR**

| | |
|---|---|
| 8.45 a.m. | early internal breakfast meeting with account teams to discuss strategy on all client brands for the week |
| 9.45 a.m. | call top monthly title regarding 4-page shoot with high-profile hair stylist that took place the day before and see how it went, how models and client were, and what products to follow up with – also set up interview with client to accompany shoot |
| 10.00 a.m. | contact accountant to discuss client's accounts and ensure they are up to date |
| 10.30 a.m. | ring around key contacts to arrange breakfast meetings for following week and discuss latest products |
| 10.45 a.m. | check press releases written by execs left in in-box on desk and go over why changes have been made |
| 11.00 a.m. | gather select members of staff to brainstorm for new business pitch and ensure there is fresh tea and chocolate biscuits for added creativity. |

| 12.00 p.m. | write up notes while they are fresh and ask press assistant to look into dates for certain events pertaining to ideas |
| 12.30 p.m. | find exciting big box on desk and then try out new spring/summer collection products that have just arrived from client. Proceed to "expertly make over" account manager with new colors – who discreetly wipes it off. |
| 12.45 p.m. | take call from client regarding outstanding coverage in Sunday supplement; discuss possible profile features in other titles |
| 1.00 p.m. | internal directors meeting to discuss staffing levels as 2 new pitches were won the week before. |
| 1.30 p.m. | have a quick power plate training session |
| 1.45 p.m. | grab quick sushi lunch at desk reading gorkana/fashion monitor/response source bulletins ensuring all possible features have been covered and review coverage that has been sent to clients |
| 2.00 p.m. | set up for new business pitch, ensure fake grass and selected "wildlife" are in place and that all technical elements have been tested; run through who is saying what |
| 2.30 p.m. | pitch takes place; goes very smoothly with all elements of brief answered |
| 3.30 p.m. | go to ad agency office to discuss new brand's PR strategy and get updated on media strategy; watch new ad campaign and view new viral campaign to be sent out the following week |
| 4.30 p.m. | afternoon tea with long lead magazine at The Wolseley, spot number of other PRs with press, wave hi; go over all new brands, products, and discuss possible feature ideas; sell in global beauty feature that will include 5 of my brands – YAY! |
| 5.30 p.m. | Go to new "hot hotel" to view rooms and potential launch venue; spot celebrity in foyer, pretend not to notice but text office to add to "celebrity |

|            | spotting list" to have a chance of winning "most spots" prize |
|------------|----------------------------------------------------------------|
| 6.00 p.m.  | wait for clients in new "hot hotel" bar and check emails on crackberry – forward those needing action to the team |
| 6.15 p.m.  | quick change and freshen up |
| 6.25 p.m.  | clients arrive and we sample cocktails while reminding them about the categories their products have been entered into and which products won what award |
| 7.00 p.m.  | go on to magazine awards and very proud client collects prize; grab a few canapés as soon as they leave the kitchen – very hungry due to very strong "hot hotel" new cocktails! |
| 8.30 p.m.  | go for dinner with client to Zuma (further celeb spots noted) and celebrate awards! |
| 11.00 p.m. | grab cab home and make mental note to leave laptop charging for client PR strategy presentation in the morning. |

## Money matters (what do PR people earn?)

Contrary to myth, PR is not a license to print money, but a competitive business sector. A few make fortunes in the consultancy sector by selling their businesses. More earn very good salaries as PR specialists in fields such as investor relations and lobbying, or by working in-house as corporate communication directors for major corporations. Most, as we shall see, earn above the national average but are far from rich, though general demand for PR has pushed salaries ahead of equivalents in journalism and many other industries that, like PR, do not insist on professional qualifications to gain entry. In short PR people tend to be better paid than their critics in the media or academia, a fact which may fuel animosity, but they do not number among the mega-rich of the contemporary world.

In the United Kingdom a communications director for a *Financial Times* top-100 company can expect to earn in excess of £200,000 per annum, plus a bonus of up to 50% of base pay.[2] In the United States the median salary for an Executive Vice President of corporate communications is $192,000.[3] Similarly the CEOs of the biggest PR consultancies can expect to earn well over £200,000 or circa $400,000, and owner-managers can pocket millions of dollars or pounds if they sell their business to one of the big groups.

For most the reality is more modest. As befits an industry that is open to anyone, does not suffer from any shortage of applicants, and does not require a degree or special training, starting salaries tend to be at the lower end of the scale. This can be as little as £14,000/$28,000 in-house and not much more in consultancy. Such sums are well below starting salaries in areas such as finance and law.

The *PR Week*/Bloom Gross Survey (see above) indicates a median annual base salary of $80,930 for all PRs and a median salary of $40,000 for those with up to two years experience. Community relations was the least well paid sector at $40,000 and reputation management the best on $115,000 per annum. However, according to the US Department for Labor (May 2006) the median annual earnings for salaried public relations specialists was only $47,350 (well below the *PR Week* figure), highlighting the difficulty of getting an accurate picture of the PR industry.[4]

In the United Kingdom the figures are broadly similar. The average salary for a 30-year-old in-house private sector press officer was just £25,000. Within consultancy the average for a 29-year-old account manager was £29,000. Not surprisingly the public sector is the worst paid. The average age of a PR manager is 39 and the average salary just £34,000.[5]

While the CIPR say 74% of people in PR are now graduates (mostly in social sciences, arts, or management studies) educational qualifications make little or no difference to earnings or job positions according to the European Communication Report 2007.[6] Bright graduates who want to make money will consider finance, the law, and management consultancy before contemplating PR. For those for whom money is not the primary motivation – or who cannot get into the better paid sectors – PR remains an attractive career option.

## The public voice of PR

One of the PR industry's peculiarities is the way it is represented in public. The industry trade associations such as the PRSA in the United States and the UK's CIPR believe it should be represented by them. It seldom is.

Apart from organizing awards, training, and urging best practice, a major part of what PR trade bodies attempt to do is deliver speeches and media statements in the hope of earning the respect due to a "profession." Spokespeople from the trade bodies flail against PR's depiction in the media and popular culture, which is often based on the role models they abhor, but barring the occasional offer of a few column inches in a serious newspaper their remarks are seldom heard beyond the four walls of PR industry events or the pages of *PR Week*. Beyond their paying customer base, the efforts of PR industry's own organizations to promote its desired self-image to the world have been ineffectual.

The problem they face, as we noted earlier, is that their statements are either seen as totally self-serving; "PR is the most important and fastest growing management discipline today"; or pompous and unbelievable: "PR has a duty to tell the truth and is about mutually beneficial relationships."

The trade bodies seldom include the high-profile political figures or the talkative and opinionated entrepreneurial heads of major consultancies among their members. Lord Bell, who probably remains the UK PR industry's biggest player, is a particular subject of the CIPR's interest and has received their highest accolade, the President's Medal for distinguished service to public relations. In the then IPR's monthly magazine, *Profile*, he explained why he has never been a member of the Institute:

> I've always been used to being a brand leader and if you're a brand leader you don't do what the competition do – so I've never joined anything. I tend to think that trade bodies are for the run-of-the-mill rather than top-end businesses – which is probably completely wrong.[7]

In practice, official PR bodies are like most trade and professional bodies, in that leading practitioners tend to concentrate on their lucrative and demanding practices, while less established figures see industry organizations as offering opportunities for self-promotion and avenues for achieving recognition. Celebrity within the circles of "official" PR, which offers numerous events and other opportunities to express views, may be a soothing substitute for stellar business success.

Those who serve as the unelected "un-official" spokespeople for PR are the kind of engaging well-connected characters described earlier in this chapter. They have their own businesses and they are opinionated, but they are seldom active members, if they are members at all, of the trade associations. Only rarely are they top people from the big consultancies or in-house PR departments. Why is this?

One obvious reason is that people in senior, established positions are less in need of a personal PR profile than the entrepreneurial individuals who own and run their own business. For example, in the United Kingdom, two of the most quoted PR people, Max Clifford and Mark Borkowski, have their names above the door. Any PR they generate is could lead to new business and hence benefit them directly. In the United States Richard Edelman, president and global CEO of top-ranking agency Edelman, which remains independent, has a high profile within the industry and beyond. This sort of profile is uncommon for heads of firms owned by big groups.

Unsurprisingly people who have the drive and ego to set up a firm bearing their name also tend to like seeing their name in lights. Those that have worked their way up the greasy corporate pole tend to be a little less extrovert and flamboyant and warier about saying something that might alienate their big corporate clients. Even the big in-house players – with a few notable exceptions – seldom get heavily involved, being either too busy or too aware of the danger of making general statements about PR that might come back to haunt them and lead to them being challenged by the media when their own corporation's PR falls short in some way. Fear of embarrassment is surely one of the main reasons that many senior PR people's public pronouncements sound so pious and platitudinous – and so unlike the engaging things they say in private.

> But the PR man, despite the often vast budgets at his command, is still looked upon with widespread skepticism. There is more suspicion than knowledge of just how he operates: his very reputation as a clever manipulator tends to frustrate his continual striving for professional recognition. It is a sorry frustration, which accounts for much of the solemn rhetoric about the "mission" of public relations.
> Irwin Ross[8]

# From PR to propaganda

## The persuasive industry's problem with definitions

We have jettisoned tradition and left the issue of definitions to Chapter 7. It is because we are confident that anyone, from members of the public to the most senior and experienced practitioner, understands what is meant by the term PR or public relations – at least in general or colloquial terms. But people have much more difficulty agreeing on a precise definition. Indeed there are estimated to be more than 500 plus definitions of PR,[1] and the fact that so many people have felt the need to try so hard to define it is telling.

First we will look at the most common definitions of PR used by the PR industry itself, then offer our own definition, and finally examine PR's relationship to propaganda.

### How the industry defines itself

In 1988, the governing body of the Public Relations Society of America – its Assembly – adopted a definition of public relations which is widely used: "Public relations helps an organization and its publics adapt mutually to each other."

The British definition devised by the Chartered Institute of Public Relations (CIPR) is different, making much play of the word "reputation":

> Public relations is about reputation – the result of what you do, what you say and what others say about you.
>
> Public relations is the discipline which looks after reputation, with the aim of earning understanding and

support and influencing opinion and behavior. It is the planned and sustained effort to establish and maintain goodwill and mutual understanding between an organization and its publics.

One of the more interesting definitions was drawn up in 1978 at the first World Assembly of Public Relations Associations (also known as the Mexican Statement).

It is the art and social science of analyzing trends, predicting their consequences, counseling organizational leaders and implementing programs of action which will serve both the organization's and the public interest.

These three definitions, covering as they do the United States, the United Kingdom, and the world, represent the official industry view. The problem with all of them is that they are not written by detached observers but by practitioners and members of trade associations who have a strong vested interest in promoting a positive view of the practice of PR. Whether consciously or not they seek to protect and boost the status of an industry which they know is often described by the general public and the media in less than flattering terms. Ironically, by defining PR in terms that many in the public find either disingenuous or actively untruthful they further damage the reputation of that which they seek to protect.

All these definitions are marred by their failure to stress the reason for public relations activity. For example, *goodwill and mutual understanding* (British definition) are not ends in themselves, but means to an end, whether it be adherence to the recommendations of a health campaign, a more productive workforce, acceptance of a new development by a local community, increased sales of goods or services, or investors buying – or at least not selling – shares in a company. PR is a purposeful activity.

The British claim that PR is about *reputation* is also misleading. There are many activities that impact on reputation that PR practitioners have little or nothing to do with. For example, PR seldom determines product performance or service delivery. So to assert that public relations is the discipline that looks after reputation is to exaggerate – it is more of an aspiration than a definition. Moreover there are clearly PR campaigns where reputation is not the central objective, for instance those encouraging changes in social behavior, or attacking government policy. Indeed all these definitions seem to exclude negative PR, although as we shall see this is a staple of political PR, as well as of the PR activities of not-for-profit organizations.

Similarly, the American view that PR is about helping an *organization and its public adapt mutually to each other* fails to describe how PR actually works and also glosses over the fact that public relations activity is generally undertaken to achieve objectives that are more specific and hard-nosed than mutual adaptation. Such language sidesteps the fact that PR is driven by its instigator, not its target. PR is not about love of mankind but a desire to achieve something for the organization paying for it. Sometimes the aim may be a noble one and be for the benefit of all mankind (although whether this is so will always be awash with value judgments), but for the most part it is not, except in the vague sense of "participating in the market place of ideas and contributing to economic growth."

The "Mexican Statement" is strong on describing what PR does or should do at the strategic level – *analyzing trends, predicting their consequences, counseling organizational leaders* – but loses focus when it says *and implementing programs.* What sort of programs? Building new factories? Creating an advertising campaign? In common with the other definitions it does not say *how* PR does what it is meant to do, nor does it acknowledge that the primary purpose is to achieve the objectives of the initiator rather than serve the public interest.

---

### Days of Wine and Roses

In this Hollywood film Jack Lemmon's PR man struggles to explain his job to his skeptical would-be father-in-law:

"Well I suppose you might say my job is sort of to help my client create a public image ... well for an example, let's say my clients, corporation x does some good ... well my job is to see that the public knows it."

His father-in-law-to-be asks your what happens if your x corporation makes a mistake and things turn out bad. The PR man responds:

"Well, er, I guess then I try and make it look not quite so bad. Well actually there's more to it than that, sir."

His fiancée tries to rescue him – "It's terrifically complicated Daddy" – but the scene concludes with the old man shaking his head and saying "I don't understand that kind of work."

## The industry's reluctance to admit the obvious

Most outsiders – and many insiders – immediately associate PR with persuasion. However persuasion is a word and an activity which is often viewed with suspicion. Throughout history many terms associated with the process of persuading fellow human beings to think or act in particular ways have acquired negative connotations. Timeless techniques of public speaking and oral argument certainly fall into this category. For example, the *Shorter Oxford English Dictionary* outlines the evolution of the meaning of *rhetoric* thus:

1. The art of using language so as to persuade or influence others
2. Orig. elegance of language. Later, language calculated to persuade or impress; freq. Derog. or joc. artificial, insincere, or extravagant language.

Webster's online dictionary also covers some of rhetoric's negative associations, citing "high flown style; excessive use of verbal ornamentation; Loud and confused and empty talk; 'mere rhetoric'."

The term *sophistry* originally referred to the approach adopted by the Sophist philosophers, but is now defined as "Specious or oversubtle reasoning, the use of intentionally deceptive arguments; casuistry."[2]

In our view PR *is* about persuading people to act (or not act) in particular ways. But for some within the industry, and particularly those who seek to explain what it is they do to the outside world, the negative aura of persuasion is a PR problem they seem unable or unwilling to tackle. Putting clear blue water between themselves and the specter of salesmanship, they distance themselves from the arts of persuasion. As one British academic wrote, "public relations is sometimes, if erroneously, seen as an instrument of persuasion."[3]

The American academics Grunig and Hunt's four models of public relations have been particularly influential. In the "public information model," practiced – they claim – by 50% of organizations, there is not necessarily any persuasive intent:

> The public relations person functions essentially as a journalist in residence, whose job it is to report objectively information about his [sic] organization to the public.

In their ideal, "two-way symmetric model," practitioners "usually use theories of communication rather than theories of persuasion."[4]

Indeed one of Grunig's conclusions is that "Public relations ... should be ethical in that it helps build caring – even loving – relationships with other individuals and groups they affect in a society."[5]

Attempts by PR people and sympathetic writers and academics to insulate public relations from the notion of persuasion fly in the face of most people's common sense – and what they have heard. For every person who has immersed themselves in a PR textbook, hundreds of thousands will have heard Edina, the PR anti-heroine of the popular TV series *Absolutely Fabulous*, say:

> I PR things. Places. Concepts. Lulu. I PR them ... I make the fabulous. I make the crap into credible. I make the dull into delicious.[6]

Not only do the defenders of PR's home-team fail in their presumed aim, protecting the reputation of public relations, but their efforts seem evasive and therefore counterproductive: the gap between common observation and reality becomes glaring and an industry which urges mutual understanding seems to be pulling its punches when discussing its own role.

The presenter of a major BBC radio program chaired a debate on the relationship between journalism and PR and afterwards commented:

I did balk at the catalogue of good deeds ascribed to PR professionals by one of the panellists: by her standards, Nelson Mandela and Mother Teresa would have struggled to qualify for admittance to the Institute for Public Relations[7].

## What *we* say PR is

The authors' definition:

> PR is the planned persuasion of people to behave in ways
> that further its sponsor's objectives. It works primarily
> through the use of media relations and other forms of
> third party endorsement.

Our definition is clear about the intent of public relations
(*persuasion*) and is unusual in that it also describes – in a way which
covers most public relations work – how it attempts to persuade:
*primarily through the use of media relations and other forms of third party
endorsement.* Third party endorsement refers to getting the support
and backing of independent voices: it is not about *you* saying you are
good (a province dominated by advertising, which pays for its own
space in the media), but getting someone else independently to say
you are good. Obtaining positive media coverage is the commonest
way in which PR achieves this.

Relating PR to its sponsor's objectives and not just to goodwill or
reputation means that we recognize not only that PR is purposeful
but that some PR is negative and seeks to undermine others. This
aspect of PR is something of a taboo and falls outside most established definitions. PR is also a *planned* activity: this helps distinguish
it, as a specialized discipline, from the other persuasive activities
which we all engage in our day-to-day lives.

This definition – a modified version of one first published in our
book *Public Relations for Asia* – has caused controversy and continues
to provoke debate. Putting aside the criticisms of those who dislike the
word *persuasion*, there are two areas of concern. First, some insist that
PR does not just persuade people to go along with an organization's
objectives but also plays an active role in defining those objectives.
The second area of controversy relates to describing media relations
as the principal, albeit not the only, tool of PR.

How far do PR people decide the purposes of the organizations
for which they work? As one prominent spokesperson for the UK
industry puts it, albeit somewhat defensively, "We're supposed
to be strategists, advisers, working in the boardroom, helping
companies get their policies right."[8] On the other hand former
UK Prime Minister Tony Blair said of his long-serving Director of

Communications, Alastair Campbell: "Alastair likes to make out he ran the show ... But the truth is I never ran any policy by him. Ever. I might have asked how something would play in the press, but never how to formulate policy."[9]

Clearly there is a big difference between policy formation and its presentation. In the United Kingdom, according to a survey by specialist headhunters Watson Helsby,[10] fewer than a third of big businesses, all quoted on the London Stock Market, had communications directors on their main, as opposed to operational, boards. Most PR people communicate policy, rather than deciding it. However proponents of PR like to portray themselves as sitting at the top table and like to claim as much power as possible, particularly as power equates to money and status. This perception is shared by critics of PR, and there has been much resentment in the United States and the United Kingdom at the power and influence of political spin doctors.

Trusted PR advisors have opportunities to exert influence – they sometimes, particularly in time of crisis, have greater access to those they are advising than anyone else, and by definition use that access to advise them on whatever are the most pressing and high-profile issues of the moment. Tony Blair spent longer each day talking to Alastair Campbell than to anyone else, including his family,[11] and yet, as the quotation above reveals, the degree to which the spin doctor affected policy – if at all – is forever a matter of dispute. However the truth remains that PR people do not lead organizations but counsel those who do.

Critics of our definition are also reluctant to admit that PR's primary tool is media relations.

Some defenders of the purity of PR – and many who are simply trying to escape some of its negative connotations – hardly ever talk about media relations. Some have even dropped the term public relations, preferring to call themselves "communications experts." Communication may be one of those purr words which have overwhelmingly positive overtones – who's against it? – but the problem is that it is a hopelessly vague term.

Communication can cover everything from a phone call between a receptionist and a customer to door drops and million dollar advertising campaigns. It is now common to have the term "communications" as part of a job title but this is a practice which could itself be seen as "another PR stunt" or "bit of spin," designed to conceal what PR people really do. Moreover PR is far from being the only way in which organizations and individuals seek to persuade people: advertising and other marketing techniques clearly play their part.

Our emphasis on media relations is important because it is the one persuasive technique which is the unchallenged preserve of PR. In contrast almost every other approach used by the industry is under-taken and can be claimed by other disciplines. Indeed, but for the need for media relations work, the PR industry in its current form would not have emerged. Although anyone may engage in media relations activity, undertaking it in a planned and deliberate way, and deriving one's livelihood from so doing, is unique to PR. Making the call to a journalist, writing a press release, arranging a press conference or handling press enquiries is something the PR person does – and other persuaders are usually happy to leave it that way. The idea of speaking to a potentially hostile journalist and being quoted – or misquoted – to an audience of millions scares many peo-ple. Moreover, many of the other activities that PR people undertake, such as organizing events and the publication of reports, have media coverage as a secondary if not primary objective.

According to an IPR survey in 1999 in the United Kingdom, media relations work accounted for 37% of PR practitioners' time. Next in order came advising management (25%), brochure/video/ print production (14%), event management (10%), and research (9%).[12] Advising management is of course seen as the most prestigious form of PR activity and is therefore likely to be overreported (it would be interesting to compare this with a survey of managements' views on what their PR people do). Moreover much of the advice given to management is likely to concern how certain policies or practices will play with the media: it would be odd if PR practitioners' advice was not closely related to their main area of activity. It is also clear that a significant proportion of the other activities can be carried out equally well, if not better, by other, non-PR, staff.

A similar message is to be found in *Unlocking the Potential of Public Relations: Developing Good Practice*, a report jointly funded by the British Government's Department of Trade and Industry and the IPR, published in November 2003. In a survey of in-house PR prac-titioners in the private sector it lists some 12 main purposes of PR, many of which include media relations activity. However of all the purposes listed "positive image in the media" and "managing issues and crises," itself an area of activity with a high media relations component, come closest to being the main rationale for PR. A "positive image in the media" is also seen by in-house practitioners and consultants as the area in which PR is most effective.[13]

Despite this the PR industry is uncomfortable with anyone emphasizing its role in media relations, preferring to emphasize other forms of communication and its overarching strategic role (strategy being one of the PR industry's favorite words). Hence the omission of media relations from all the other definitions of which we are aware. Edward Bernays, speaking toward the end of his life, was particularly grandiloquent: "We've [speaking of himself!] had no direct contact with the mass media for about fifty years."[14] This may sometimes be true for those involved in financial or public affairs campaigns, but even they have to use the media as well as other third parties such as analysts and political insiders. Few modern PR campaigns lack a media element and most have media coverage at their heart. Indeed the PR industry's reluctance to admit to the centrality of media relations also flies in the face of the understanding of PR in wider society. To most outsiders PR is forever, and overwhelmingly, associated with journalism and the media, with press releases and press conferences.

This contradiction can partly be explained by the natural urge of every industry or profession for self-aggrandizement, but there are other reasons why PR people want to play down media relations. Too often media relations work is seen as a set of tactical devices which are beneath the dignity of an industry with higher pretensions; it is associated with *saying* rather than *doing*. There is also a sense in which PR practitioners, with an ill-defined role in the lives of the organizations for which they work, crave the kudos of a central decision-making role. A desire for more acknowledgment from the higher echelons of business runs through many public utterances by PR people. They want to be more than a means to an end, and to be business gurus and management consultants rather than mere media handlers and intermediaries. There is also a skeleton in the cupboard: PR has press agentry in its family tree. Given press agentry's seedy associations with the hucksters of early twentieth-century America, this is something PR would rather overlook. As Irwin Ross observed 50 years ago, "Since few practitioners like to be called 'press agents', success is often measured in the amount of time one talks to one's clients – and not to the press."[15]

Playing down the role of media relations in PR is also a way of distancing the industry from its awkward relationship with journalism. It is worth noting that journalists and many others in the media have the same sort of problems defining what they do. Much as they like to use terms such as "the pursuit of the truth" and "protecting the people from the rich and powerful," the reality is that most journalism is about providing information and entertainment in a way that sells a media product. Few journalists will ever, in the course of their careers, expose a major wrongdoing or reveal an important truth that would otherwise have remained concealed.

### Is propaganda different?

Propaganda is probably the most noxious epithet to be hurled at public relations and the other arts of persuasion. This is ironic as propaganda has – depending on one's point of view – very respectable origins. The *Sacra Congregatio de Propaganda Fide*, a committee of Roman Catholic cardinals responsible for overseas missions, was founded in 1622 by Pope Gregory XV. It was only later that distaste for the use of professional techniques to put across information and promote ideas lent the word its pejorative meaning.[16]

Bernays said that it was as a result of the odium associated with the use of propaganda in the First World War that he adopted the title of counselor in public relations.[17] Certainly the First World War did much to give propaganda a bad name. Wartime depictions of Germans as baby-killers and violators of nuns contributed to America's involvement in the conflict, and yet many of the claims turned out to be baseless. It also made it hard at the war's end to persuade people that a harsh peace might not be in anyone's long-term interests. Then, in the interwar years organizations such as the Institute for Propaganda Analysis, run by a penitent former wartime propagandist, revealed the depth of deception used during the war to manage Allied public opinion. As a result attitudes against propaganda hardened, which ironically made it difficult for people to believe initial reports of Nazi atrocities.

But what is propaganda? Is it just public relations for a distasteful cause, or is it distinct?

PR academics Grunig and Hunt acknowledge the existence of propaganda in their four models of public relations but dismiss it as simple "source to recipient" communication. The most advanced and virtuous of their models is called "two-way symmetric" and involves achieving mutual understanding based on negotiation and compromise.[18] Although they advance no evidence to support their claims, their views have had considerable influence in PR's academic enclaves (perhaps for the dubious reason that in the world of higher education any theory is better than none).[19] Their thinking would leave most real-life practitioners bemused, but it is not without consequences. Indeed it seems academic isolation coupled with intellectual insecurity has allowed idealistic but suspect thinking such as that of Grunig and Hunt to flourish unchecked, without proper scrutiny.

One problem is that the allegedly "two-way symmetrical" communication between an organization and its publics will always be paid for by one side, and since the organization is the paymaster it is hard to see the exchange as other than *a*symmetrical: its interests come first. But on the other hand some form of asymmetrical two-way communication is always the aim of intelligent propagandists, not for ethical reasons but simply because listening to and understanding your intended audiences makes communication more effective. Goebbels – the evil genius of propaganda *par excellence* – understood this and impressed upon his staff the importance of gauging the public mood in Germany.[20]

Some seek to establish a clear distinction between propaganda and public relations by adopting another approach we have encountered. It is to try to claim that, unlike propaganda, PR is not about persuasion but, at least in its ideal form, it is about "mutual understanding."

Others attempt to establish a distinction by saying that PR and propaganda serve different causes. PR is depicted as serving praiseworthy, legitimate causes, whereas propaganda is associated with war and the less acceptable ends of the political spectrum. Although many people instinctively refer to communications that they dislike as "propaganda," it only needs a moment's thought to see how subjective and riddled with value judgments this approach must be. As Taithe and Thornton note, it has the interesting side effect that

> Propaganda is often most fully discussed in counter-propaganda. Denouncing the other's devious techniques and lack of credibility, while displaying similar methods, makes this a paradoxical and in some ways self-undermining process.[21]

Nor is propaganda necessarily about war or politics. Not only do its origins lie in religion, but the term's usage remains broad. The literary example provided by the Shorter Oxford English Dictionary is "An active propagandist for the conservation of the forests."

Then there is the issue of the truth. Certainly propaganda is often seen as all but coterminous with lying, while public relations trade bodies cite adherence to the truth as articles in their professional codes.[22] But what truth is, and whether it is practical for PR people to tell it all the time, is a thorny issue as we saw in Chapter 4.

Moreover, lying is far from *de rigueur* for the intelligent propagandist. Many lies may be told, but Goebbels' diaries reveal numerous instances of him arguing with his colleagues about their simplistic desire to claim false successes and deny real reversals.[23] The reason was not moral squeamishness, but rather one of efficacy: for him lies were often in the long run the stupidest and least effective form of publicity.[24] Lying about things which are glaringly obvious – or soon will be – is usually ill-advised: the propagandist would squander their credibility. At best the intelligent propagandist can exert some control over bad news, by selecting the exact moment for its announcement and by managing the way it is revealed. PR people often explain the need to tell the truth in terms of the importance of maintaining their credibility with journalists, and here public relations and propaganda come closer than PR people might like. PR's attitude to the truth is conditioned by practicality and the maximizing of advantage as much as by moral imperatives.

*     *     *

Scholars of propaganda have fewer problems as they are engaged in the study of a discipline and not its promotion (or indeed its denigration). So, for example, to cite one prominent authority:

> In accordance with established practice among scholars of mass persuasion, the word *propaganda* is used ... not in the popular pejorative sense, but as a specific term to describe the act of mass persuasion.[25]

For Professor Philip Taylor:

> By propaganda, then, I mean the *deliberate* attempt to persuade people to think and behave *in a desired way* ... Public relations is a related communicative process

designed to enhance the relationship between an organization and the public and, as such, is a branch of propaganda, albeit a nicer way of describing it.[26]

The idea that propaganda and public relations are to some degree interchangeable terms helps explain the way in which American pioneers of public relations such as Ivy Lee[27] and Carl Byoir[28] were able to work for the Nazis, and how, or so the story goes, Goebbels made use of Bernays' writings.[29] It was presumably the US PR industry which Goebbels had in mind when he said: "After the war I'll go to America. There at least they will appreciate a propaganda genius, and pay him accordingly!"[30]

So what, if anything, really distinguishes public relations from propaganda? Our contention is that there are no real moral distinctions: both practices are essentially *a*moral, capable of serving any cause. However there are some practical differences. The ubiquity of propaganda as a term arises from the fact that it does not just describe a debating technique or particular mode of persuasion such as media relations. Instead, rooted in the work of the Roman Catholic Church, an organization with universalist claims which had every known means of persuasion at its disposal, it is all-encompassing.

Thus propaganda is perhaps best seen as describing the orchestra of persuasion. Propagandists exploit all possibilities for influencing human thought and action. These overlap but include education, all forms of art, architecture, interior design, literature, music, clothing, advertising, speeches, ritual, ceremonies, parades, sport ... anything and anywhere where the human senses can be engaged in a way that enables people to influence others. It is telling that the sheer scope and scale of the levers available to the propagandist mean that in practice full control over them resides with the ultimate leader – a Hitler or a Stalin – and not with any subordinate. Hitler, who started his rise to power in the Nazi Party as the person in charge of propaganda, never allowed anyone else to conduct the full orchestra: even Goebbels' role was carefully circumscribed. Propaganda work in the Soviet system was also carefully parceled out.

Public relations might have grown to be a significant section within the orchestra, but other sections remain important. PR may try to use other propaganda techniques as it pursues its persuasive goals, but it has a different history – one that contributed to its rise as distinct discipline during the last century. PR can be seen historically as a response, initially by commercial interests and governments, to the rising power of the mass media. As newspaper circulations rose and news agendas developed to include more critical reportage, early PR practitioners sought to ward off or at least minimize hostile coverage. They also sought to go on the offensive, promoting positive stories on behalf of those employing them, thereby using the communications potential of the mass media to support their marketing and other corporate objectives. Thus PR's bedrock was press handling or media relations.

This need for PR arose because of the freedoms enjoyed by the media and a perception that independent mass media were of critical importance to the fates of even the most powerful groups in society. The media's freedom might not be perfect, but organizations could not – and cannot – be certain about the kind of coverage they would – or will – receive. Hostile stories remain a possibility, and the "good news" stories which organizations want to promote can be ignored or downplayed by media which prize their independence.

## PR: a symptom of freedom

Although there are countries today with controlled media that have PR industries (albeit small and unsophisticated ones), any authoritarian state with a command economy and directly controlled media has little need for PR: its leaders can already be certain of what will appear in the media. Instead, in so far as such countries practice PR their focus is on other countries, where they cannot enjoy the same confidence about what will be said. It is with this in mind that some of the world's most deplorable regimes have invested in PR in America and Europe. As long as journalists enjoy a measure of independence PR people are in demand, since the nature of media coverage remains a gamble. Thus PR may be predominantly a tool of the already powerful, but, regardless of the causes it serves, it is also a symptom of freedom, used by all sections in society (even if the not-for-profit sector is particularly reluctant to call what they do PR).

In contrast propaganda is an older and perhaps grander activity. Its origins long predate the establishment of the mass media, and the emergence of modern ideals of free expression. Although it has adapted itself to new circumstances – the use of PR in modern, heavily mediated societies such as Britain and America is an obvious example – the propagandistic ideal remains one of controlling all debate, dominating all media, and excluding alternative voices. Indeed while propagation of the message lies at the heart of propaganda, censorship and repression are equally important. Although no monopoly over information flows is perfect – the Soviet Union continued to have its *samizdat*, for example – the aim is to make control of communication as watertight as possible. PR people may occasionally have ambitions in this direction, and use a range of techniques to suppress unwanted reports, but the unhappy fate of countless governments and big companies in all democratic countries demonstrates that they lack full control over what is said about their clients or employers.

Public Relations can therefore be differentiated from propaganda in three ways:

1. It has far fewer levers of influence to pull on.
2. It exists in conditions where many competing persuasive messages are communicated.
3. The public relations practitioner, unlike the propagandist, does not have effective powers of censorship or any lasting control over the media.

Public Relations flourishes and grows in democracies and free markets. There is little place for it in dictatorships or command economies.

# CHAPTER 8

# Professional, but never a profession

## Playing the piano in a brothel

> When I started off in public relations, it was a business that people went into because they weren't good at anything else ... I thought that I'd like to start my own business. And as I wasn't very good at anything, I decided I'd better start a PR firm.[1]

So said Lord Chadlington, a grandee of the British PR industry, founder of the international PR firm Weber Shandwick, and member of the upper house of the UK legislature. A lot of people in public relations still share his view. All you need to get started is a desk, a computer, a phone, and "self confidence, a degree of social skill and an interest in the media."[2]

But despite this ease of entry, professional status has been a shimmering goal for some PR practitioners since the industry's beginnings. It is not difficult to understand why.

A proper profession with highly regulated entry and enforceable codes of practice and conduct offers a number of attractive benefits for its members. Perhaps most importantly, it is effectively a closed shop. By restricting the number of practitioners fees can be kept high, thus defying the natural tendency of an open market to force rates down and/or to cause employers to shed surplus labor. Professions also offer high social status. They are seen as vocations or callings which place social ideals above grubby commercial advantage. Nonprofessionals have to sell themselves while true professionals are sought out, or so many believe (in the United Kingdom this was reflected, until recent times, in the way many professions were not allowed to advertise their services). The truth may of course be different.

A lot of social anxiety surrounds professions. The humor of many ethnic groups is particularly rich with jokes about mothers hoping that their children will enter the professions or at least marry into them. Medicine, law, or even accountancy are seen as attractive, safe occupations. But we are unaware of any jokes about ambitious mothers longing for their child to go into PR! Indeed one of the few jokes about PR involves a young man being asked what he does for a living. His response is: "I work in public relations. But please don't tell my mother. She thinks I play the piano in a brothel."

**The other PR joke**

A PR consultant has a heart attack and finds himself at the gates of heaven talking to St Peter.

"St Peter, there must have been a mistake. I'm only 40. I'm sure I'm not meant to be here yet. I still have important work to do."

St Peter is sympathetic and goes off to check the records on the celestial computer. A few minutes later he returns looking a little bemused.

"It's a mistake isn't it?" says the PR consultant.

"Well," says St Peter, "According to the time you have charged your clients you are 83 years old."

## What is a profession?

Since professions occupy an exalted place in people's social mind-maps it is unsurprising that people working in an industry which so often sees itself as being concerned with reputation should want to attain this coveted status. But in its strict sense a profession has a number of characteristics which PR lacks – and which PR will never acquire.

First, members of a profession have to master a substantial body of specialist knowledge, usually well beyond that required for a first degree. This involves prolonged study over a number of years and a process of rigorous examination. It is only when such study is successfully completed, often in conjunction with extensive supervised work experience, that individuals are entitled to membership of the professional body.

Second, membership of the professional body is a formal requirement for anyone who wishes to carry out the profession's core functions. For example, non-lawyers have no right of audience in law courts, and similarly certain functions are reserved for doctors and accountants.

Finally, the membership of a profession is policed. Professional bodies concern themselves with members' ethics and set standards which go beyond simple adherence to the law. Transgressors may be disciplined or even expelled from the profession (which of course means they can no longer perform the functions reserved for members of the professional body).

## Is PR a profession?

For all the talk about PR becoming a profession (often admittedly with a hint of *manana* about it), there is seldom any hard thought about what this would entail.

First, it would be hard to argue that PR possessed anything resembling the substantial, agreed body of specialist knowledge which characterizes well-established professions. A simple book count is not enough: the quality and rigor of the literature, and the acceptance of its importance by those working in the field, are also key issues. PR is essentially an art not a science, and in so far as there are iron rules they do not begin to amount to the body of knowledge which trainee lawyers or accountants, let alone doctors, have to master. Such PR books as there are tend to duck and dive around the more sensitive and interesting aspects of PR practice.

For example, in our recent book *Public Relations for Asia* we describe the "black arts" which PR practitioners sometimes use to try to suppress or minimize bad news about the organizations they serve. These are well documented and undoubtedly form a major part of what the most senior PR people do, but as far as we know they have been passed over in other textbooks because they do not conform to the industry's desired public image. Moreover, if one took a generous view of the growing number of PR textbooks, the fact that they remain unread by so many working in, or entering, the industry makes it hard to consider them a foundation for the professional practice of PR.

Second, even if one argues that such a body of knowledge exists, there is no need to demonstrate one's mastery of it in order to practice.

In most countries there is no barrier to anyone offering PR services. Anyone can set up a PR consultancy, and organizations are free to employ whomsoever they wish to carry out PR duties. Closed entry has been attempted in some places, but we doubt its effectiveness.[3]

## More problems with definitions

The looseness of definition is a serious handicap to any bid to establish PR on a proper professional footing. For example, to try to preclude anyone who was not a PR practitioner from involvement in something as vague as "reputation management" – which overlaps with advertising, not to mention general management functions – would be unworkable. Nonetheless this is the preferred definition of one of the main industry bodies (see Chapter 7).

As an alternative, if one sought to define specific roles which PR people – and only PR people – could undertake, other problems emerge. Would only PR people be allowed to contact the media, or issue press releases (however they might be defined) – surely an impractical idea that would be opposed by journalists and fall foul of the most basic concepts of human rights? Would non-PR people have to put the phone down if contacted by a journalist? What would happen to the community group that springs up to oppose the building of a new road? Would they be unable to contact the media unless they had a "qualified" PR practitioner? Would the small start-up business with a great idea be forced to spend funds hiring a "professional PR" rather than being able to go direct to the media? And what of those aspects of public relations which do not involve media relations? It only takes a moment's thought to see that it would be impractical to prevent unqualified people engaging in "internal communications" within organizations.

Failing that, could the term "Public Relations" be protected? In theory, yes: individuals or firms who were not members of the relevant professional bodies could be prevented from using the term to describe themselves and their work, and made to remove it from their stationery, brochures, and websites. But in practice many of them would not be too bothered. They have often minimized, or even avoided, the use of the term, and would be happy to continue using some of the other titles mentioned in this book. Protecting the term "public relations," but not the practice, would be a rather hollow victory.

## The role of trade bodies

Ease of entry into PR is one of the things that make it so attractive as a career. Not for the PR practitioner years of late night study and examinations. Instead it is highly competitive industry that depends on the marketplace – and to some degree critical journalists – to control and measure its performance. Anyone can try their hand at PR but the test of whether they succeed is a business one: there is no professional body to tilt the market in their favor. Most industry bodies have only a small percentage of practitioners as members. In the United States the PRSA has 31,000 members out of an esti-mated 240,000 working in PR (circa 13%). In the United Kingdom the CIPR – the largest "professional" body outside the United States – has around 8,000 members (although this includes many students) in an industry said to have around 48,000 practitioners (circa 16%).

Formal regulation by the industry's trade bodies – even among the minority of PR practitioners who elect to join them – has proved to be difficult. There is an enormous number of codes of conduct – national, European, international. The Global Alliance for Public Relations and Communication Management – an alliance of trade bodies rather than individuals – has the objective of creating "one profession-one voice," but has got little further than exhorting practitioners to be honest.

There are four major problems with enforcing professional PR standards.

### How is quality defined?

Given the lack of a robust, generally accepted body of knowledge it would be hard to demonstrate that the quality of PR advice has fallen below acceptable professional standards. Is a good press release one that gets good coverage and is one that does not a bad one? A great story that is badly written may still get coverage and vice versa. There would be little value in meaningless bureaucratic regulations stipu-lating that, for example, press releases must be double spaced and have a date at the top. The media – who use (or more often ignore) press releases – and the people who pay for them operate an effective market in determining quality.

Similarly, it is difficult to judge the quality of advice. The practice of public relations is not a precise science. Advice is based on judgments that depend (1) on the quality of the information provided in the first instance; (2) circumstances that can change rapidly; and, (3) the experience and knowledge of the advisor. Many variables are outside of the control of the PR practitioner: anyone doing marketing PR for an ice-cream company would relish a spell of hot weather! One problem lies in the fact that there is a tendency for PR people to overclaim when something has gone well and then be surprised when they are asked to take the blame when things do not go well. As the authors know only too well, judges of PR awards find it difficult to agree on what is best and worthy of winning. By the same token they would find it difficult to judge what is so poor as to merit the ultimate sanction of exclusion from the profession. It is hardly surprising that there are very few examples of practitioners being disciplined. Indeed, as L'Etang observed, many of the disciplinary cases that have been brought in the United Kingdom seem to be more about professional vendettas than raising standards.[4]

This is not to say that PR bodies do not – very occasionally – discipline members. But investigations are not only rare, they seldom lead to action, and when action is taken it is rarely stern. Such cases usually involve public actions where the *prima facie* case is overwhelming. The most notorious recent example is that of Murray Harkin, the erstwhile business partner of Sophie Wessex (daughter-in-law of the Queen of England), who was forced to resign from the IPR after he was exposed by a *News of the World* reporter allegedly offering to arrange sex parties for clients. The evidence was taped.[5] Some five years later he is back in business running an agency called EP (Entertainment People).

### What is truth?

Much of what is deemed to be ethically dubious about PR practice arises from private conversations: proving exactly what happened is often very difficult. Where there are serious allegations of unethical practice the laws of fraud or defamation are generally seen by the victims as the appropriate means of stopping and punishing the perpetrator – although, interestingly, we found it hard to find many examples. One of the few recent instances involved superstar actress Nicole Kidman who was in a dispute with the British newspaper *The Daily Telegraph* and PR firm Exposure over claims that she used a perfume other than Chanel. It is understood that both Exposure and the *Telegraph* ended up out of pocket.[6]

Many of the codes talk about the need to be truthful, but as we have seen in Chapter 4 truth is a much more slippery concept than people like to pretend. The selection of some facts over others can be a kind of falsehood, and most honest PR people will admit to telling "white lies." Can trade bodies expect to survive if they expel members who deny boardroom splits to probing journalists? Boardrooms, like governments, are often divided on issues. The media love this sort of conflict, but if PR people always admitted to it, the stuff of business and government would grind to a halt. Does a PR person representing a public figure have an absolute duty to tell the truth to a journalist who asks an irrelevant and intrusive question about their client's private life?

## Regulator or protector?

Trade, as opposed to professional, bodies are always anxious to retain existing members and recruit more as membership subscriptions are their main source of income – and membership is voluntary. They do so by advancing existing and potential members interests. There can be a conflict of interest between this and the aim of raising standards and regulating behavior. Groucho Marx may have said he wouldn't want to a join a club that would have him as a member, but few people are likely to flock to join a club that makes it difficult to get in and keeps on chucking people out – unless of course membership of the club turns on the tap of wealth and prestige!

So for all the talk about the need for codes of ethics, the reality is different. The Public Relations Society of America, driven by similar imperatives to the CIPR, pays lip service to the ideal:

> Ethical practice is the most important obligation of a PRSA member. We view the Member Code of Ethics as a model for other professions, organizations, and professionals.

But on the same page adds:

> Emphasis on enforcement of the Code has been eliminated.[7]

The reasons for this are outlined in an article available on the PRSA website entitled "PRSA Code of Ethics Moves from Enforcement to *Inspiration*" (our italics).[8] The PRSA realized that the code was unenforceable. There had been only 4 cases of formal sanctions over a period of 50 years.

The criticism that professional bodies protect their members can be, and is, leveled at some other recognized professional bodies, although most seem to discipline more members than the CIPR.[9] For example the medical profession in the United Kingdom gets around the problem in a different way:

> The General Medical Council (GMC) was established under the Medical Act of 1858. We have strong and effective legal powers designed to maintain the standards the public have a right to expect of doctors. We are not here to protect the medical profession – their interests are protected by others. Our job is to protect patients.[10]

Hearings about doctors accused of professional malpractice are in public,[11] something which many would argue forms an indispensable part of any fair system of adjudication, enabling justice to be seen to be done. The same is not true of the CIPR which – ironically for an organization which often extols transparency in communication – operates a closed disciplinary system:

> All complaints remain confidential. Announcement of a complaint outcome is at the discretion of the Professional Practices Committee and subject to the endorsement of the Council.[12]

### Ease of entry

An irony which sheds further light on the gulf between PR and recognized professions is that the PR industry, often seen as being at loggerheads with journalism, is littered with ex-journalists, people who in theory have a distinct professional background. From Alastair Campbell, former spin doctor to British Prime Minister Tony Blair, to Tony Snow, the former Fox TV anchor, there are countless examples of journalists who have made the move, at all levels.

The vast majority of such journalists has not previously worked in PR and has seldom bothered to obtain PR qualifications (or join PR's trade bodies). This pattern is so commonplace that people pay it little heed. It emphasizes the real importance the PR industry attaches to understanding how the media operates, for while PR people with prior working experience come from a range of backgrounds none compares in importance with journalism.

The desire and claim to be a proper distinct profession is undermined by the ability of people from a distinct occupation to move freely into public relations at the most senior of levels, frequently overtaking those who have spent their working lives in PR. The equivalent would be unthinkable in the case of recognized professions. Imagine an outsider suddenly becoming a doctor! And yet journalists frequently become prominent public relations practitioners overnight. It seems to undercut the notion that there is a major, distinct body of knowledge which is unique to PR.

## Not a profession, but trying hard

The difficult issues described above are normally fudged in PR textbooks and the public statements of those – in reality a rather small group – who seek to speak for the industry. They excuse weaknesses on the grounds that things are changing or are about to change: PR's apologists are always keen on *manana*. But there is no doubting the desire of a section of the PR industry to be taken seriously – and professional recognition is seen as key to that.

If on the other hand PR is viewed as a business activity, measured by amounts of money made, the crude but objective yardstick of commercial achievement, then the laurels in the United Kingdom would pass to people such as Lord Bell, Mrs Thatcher's former PR guru and Chairman of the UK's largest PR group; Lord Chadlington, founder of Shandwick and now chairman of the rapidly growing Huntsworth group of PR companies; or Alan Parker, the immensely rich Chairman and founder of Brunswick, the financial PR specialists. Interestingly none has taken any active part in the work of the CIPR or the Public Relations Consultants Association. (If one gave weight to growth rates then the heads of some younger, thrusting consultancies would enter the picture as well.)

For those in a smaller line of business, creating noise is part of their marketing strategy – a way of attracting attention, highlighting the services they offer and engaging in networking. But in the bigger game of public relations establishing a high public profile often offers limited benefits or can be counterproductive. The risks are high. Those who advise others on media relations are not always good interviewees or spokespeople themselves – and yet being seen to perform badly in one's chosen area of expertise is potentially bad for business. Often those paying for PR do not want a high public profile. Their target audiences are narrow, and while they use PR they want it to be as invisible as possible. It is no coincidence that Brunswick, the most successful consultancy in the United Kingdom in financial terms, has traditionally adopted a very low profile.

*   *   *

One justification for the continuance of traditional professions is that the quality standards they impose – usually based on clear empirical evidence – protect the public from potentially catastrophic abuses of power. Poor legal practice can lead to false imprisonment; poor accountancy to bankruptcy and economic collapse; poor architecture to buildings falling down; and poor medicine to death. The consequences of poor PR are seldom so serious and are quickly corrected by media attack or the mechanisms of the market.

There is a danger of PR wanting to have its cake and eat it. Sometimes it seems it wants to be seen as both a creative industry and a profession. However the unfettered creativity which PR values is something which most professions circumscribe. Interestingly PR's creative cousins in the advertising industry seem less insecure: they have settled for creativity and are largely unbothered about their lack of professional status.

We have no doubt that PR will continue to become increasingly professional in the sense that training and education will continue to improve and standards of best practice will become more commonplace and raise the bar of performance for all. Trade associations have and will continue to play an important role in this. What will not happen – and nor do we think it desirable – is that PR will become a profession operating a closed shop and excluding those without special degrees or qualifications. Indeed it would be an ironic move at a time when many traditional professions are increasingly subject to market forces.

CHAPTER 9

# PR in the not-for-profit sector

## The love of PR that dare not speak its name

PR is often attacked as the handmaiden of big business and government. It is a familiar theme, but it is time to turn the tables by looking at other users of PR. Governments and big companies, even multinationals, are hardly new phenomena, but to a large extent international nongovernmental organizations (NGOs) are. Whereas in 1956 an estimated 985 NGOs were internationally active, today the number is estimated to be around 44,000 – a figure that excludes the millions of NGOs that only operate at a national level.[1]

Well-known NGOs or pressure groups such as Greenpeace and Amnesty International have come from nowhere to become global "super-brands" which compare in prominence with major multinational corporations. They share with big business an ability to leap borders and operate internationally. Worldwide such organizations employ an estimated 19 million people, and enjoy an annual income of $1,100 billion.[2] But orthodox employment figures grossly understate the position. NGOs generate enormous amounts of volunteer support. A recent estimate suggests that in the United States alone NGOs mobilize 20 billion volunteer hours "worth" one quarter of a trillion dollars a year.[3]

NGOs live and breathe PR, for, although they seldom use the term, that is what their campaigning and activism amounts to. Some NGOs are engaged in service delivery but many of the best-known ones simply seek to advance an argument or promote a cause. Indeed great campaigning NGOs such as Amnesty and Greenpeace are the purest PR vehicles one could hope to find. Unlike governments, which have to provide services to their citizens, and companies, which depend on the profitable delivery of goods and services, such NGOs can concentrate on campaigning. Thus while Greenpeace makes its case about the environment, its adversaries such as BP and Shell devote most of their resources to extracting, refining, and distributing oil. The fact that NGOs employ many fewer staff is deceptive: those they do employ are overwhelmingly committed to what amounts to PR work.

It might be argued that determining the purpose of an NGO may go beyond the formal remit of PR – Greenpeace's precise stance on a range of issues, or Amnesty's decision to campaign against the death penalty are examples of technically – and morally – determined decision-making. Even then PR perhaps has more bearing than NGOs care to admit as the organizations consider how their stance will play with their current and potential supporters.

However once the NGOs' purposes are determined PR takes charge (advertising and sales promotion may be part of the persuasive mix, but in the NGO field PR is normally to the fore). The process is circular. Funds are raised in order to conduct media relations campaigns, to lobby, to stage events – in short to further the NGO's campaigning objectives and – if all goes well and the NGO is seen as successful – it will be able to raise more funds and recruit more staff and volunteers.

## PR for the industries of conscience

It could be argued that NGOs do sell a product – that, as what have been called "industries of conscience" – they "sell" their donors and volunteers that most delicate of luxury goods, a contented conscience. (It should be emphasized that this dispassionate analysis of one of the core functions of NGOs does not impugn their virtue: responding to one's conscience can be an excellent thing, and there are many NGOs whose objectives most of us would wholeheartedly endorse.) However this means that NGOs are engaged in a particularly sophisticated transaction, which most participants would rather not see as a transaction at all and where no tangible goods or conventional services change hands. It is one that requires lashings of good public relations. The message is subtle: customers have both to experience a contented afterglow after contributing money or time – so that they become "repeat customers" and advocates for the brand – and at the same time to feel they are acting altruistically. Much of the credibility and influence of campaigning NGOs derive from their perceived altruism: they are not serving vested interests in the way that trade unions or trade associations do.

As the NGO field has grown bigger and more successful, campaigning NGOs have become more and more akin to big companies, sharing many of their techniques as they seek to "sell" their products. They employ highly professional staff who move around the sector. Good career prospects within a vibrant "industry" mean that NGOs can attract increasingly high quality staff. There is even an intriguing crosscurrent whereby NGO veterans sell their credibility, experience and skills back to the private sector as it seeks to fight off challenges from NGOs. Rival NGOs compete with each other for staff, funding, and media coverage – discreetly but ruthlessly (one expert described them to the authors as fighting like ferrets in a sack) – in a way that any free marketeer would recognize.

In implementing their PR programs NGOs also compete for celebrities and media attention, just like their corporate counterparts. However they do so with much more of a following wind from the media. The PR techniques and the messages they seek to put across are seldom challenged, while the motives and actions of their corporate or political counterparts are always suspect and often pilloried. The notion that NGO actions are selfless, in contrast to profit-obsessed corporations or power-hungry politicians, is pervasive, and is reflected in the greater degree of trust they attract. It gives them enormous PR clout, and so it is certainly time for critics of the role of PR in contemporary societies to subject NGOs to more searching examination.

In 2006 a Greenpeace report about the consequences of the Chernobyl nuclear accident in 1986 produced headlines such as "CHERNOBYL'S REAL DEATH TOLL 90,000, SAYS GREENPEACE." In fact, as Nick Davies argues, this and other stories were "an inaccurate account of a Greenpeace press release which was in itself an inaccurate account of the organization's own report which was itself somewhat problematic." These flaws failed to inhibit the media story.[4]

> As Davies puts it elsewhere, "Greenpeace is particularly skilled
> at creating pseudo-incidents."[5]

## NGOs in conflict

Sympathetic observers overlook the fact that NGOs may be created
and run by flawed and ambitious individuals with their own agendas.
No-one can agree with everything they say: NGOs are frequently at
odds with each other about both the ends they are pursuing and the
means they use to pursue them. There may be fundamental disagreement over issues such as the Middle East, birth control, or abortion,
or the tension may be less obvious, such as between those seeking to
preserve the countryside and those seeking affordable housing. As we
have seen elsewhere, even if there is broad agreement on objectives
there may be fierce disagreement about the detail: environmental
groups, for example, while sharing a concern about global warming, may disagree about the value of, and risk associated with, wind
farms, tidal power, biofuels, and carbon offsetting schemes.

The PR techniques NGOs use should also be subject to greater
scrutiny. They seem free to use a range of publicity stunts – up to and
including breaking the law – for publicity purposes. Not only does
this give them considerable advantages, but it leads to them making
emotional appeals of a kind which many critics of PR deplore – it is,
after all, easy to lose sight of cool rational argument founded on careful
assessment of the evidence amidst an eye-catching photo-opportunity
or emotional soundbite. The fact that these stunts are often reported
unexamined by the media frequently compounds the problem, and
indeed people who would be highly critical of emotional appeals in
other contexts suspend their judgment in the case of NGOs. NGOs also
use their moral authority in another way. They launch direct attacks
on other organizations in a way which is rare in commercial PR (most
companies fear that they risk damaging their own reputations as well
as those of their sector if they launch direct attacks on competitors).
Attacks of this kind by NGOs are inherently more newsworthy than
the "good news" stories companies seek to generate.

## Propaganda of the deed

As mentioned, the peculiar status of NGOs enables some campaigning
organizations flagrantly to break the law as part of their campaigning

activity in ways which would be unthinkable in private sector or government PR. Such tactics – often involving acts such as trespass, obstruction, and criminal damage – fit all the criteria for news-worthiness, and tend to be viewed benignly by the media and public opinion. If the cause is, for example, an environmental one – and everyone is in favor of protecting the environment – there is often little reasoned critique of the campaign. But some NGOs go further, with, for instance, animal rights or antiabortion groups overstepping the bounds of nonviolence and threatening or launching attacks on people and property. At this extreme point NGO activity can shade into terrorism. Indeed terrorism itself, once called the "Propaganda of the Deed," can be usefully defined as an extreme form of PR. In essence it is about garnering publicity and effecting change by sending messages. Terrorist outrages are the most extreme form of media relations, but rely on publicity to achieve their desired goals as they do not of themselves achieve the traditional military objectives of defeating armies or conquering territory.

A final, seldom mentioned problem arises from NGOs' lack of accountability and transparency. Democratic governments regularly submit themselves for reelection, and the boards of public companies can also be voted out. In both cases this ultimate control is supported by all kinds of reporting requirements, with large amounts of information being made publicly available and subject to independent checks of various kinds. Information and rival views are appraised and vigorously discussed in the media. The position in the NGO sector is much more complicated. There is no universal standard of accountability, nor is it always clear how decisions are reached: big NGOs are not democracies where members can determine policies. The information made available may be patchy: some NGOs may be subject to charity law, but others are not, and large NGOs frequently operate across different jurisdictions. Nor is a broadly sympathetic media applying much vigilance to the activities of NGOs. Those hostile to the PR industry tend to abandon their critical facilities when it comes to the PR activities of NGOs. Overall it seems that while many NGOs seek greater transparency from governments and corporations they are not always so keen to expose themselves to scrutiny.

Some in NGOs will argue that the noble end justifies the means. The media would do well to question more often if this is always true.

# CHAPTER 10

# Internal communications

## A case of PR or propaganda?

You may not have given it much thought, but if you have worked in a modern organization of any size you will have encountered internal communications. It may be as simple as a staff newsletter, an intranet site, or internal emails. It may involve direct personal contact – speeches, meetings, and training sessions. It may not be about words at all, but be expressed through office furniture, corporate uniforms and dress regulations, art, music or muzak, even the architecture and décor of the organization's buildings. The list is endless and covers every interface between individuals and their employers. Organizations have always practiced employee communications, just as they have always, often unwittingly, practiced some form of PR. What is different today is that internal communications has increasingly become something which is planned and deliberate and involves the work of specialist staff (rather like PR itself). Indeed some argue that it will account for a growing share of what the PR industry does.

> According to the founder of one of the world's largest PR consultancies, Harold Burson of Burson-Marsteller, "major corporations' demand for advice on internal comms is likely to drive agency growth more than anything else." Such work accounted for 12–15% of the global consultancy's activity, a figure he expected to grow.[1]

Since the flow of information and opinion is the lifeblood of any organization, internal communications need to be distinguished from routine communication. It is best understood as a focused activity which is separate from, even if it complements, normal flows of communication within an organization (such as those between managers and staff, or among colleagues). To this end specialist staff employ a range of techniques. Indeed large organizations may control extensive media empires of their own, devoted to communicating with internal audiences, using dedicated television, radio, and intranet sites as well as other digital and print media.

We have seen that PR people sometimes agonize about the relationship between public relations and propaganda. Internal communications is the branch of the modern PR industry that best realizes the propagandists' dream. Unlike media relations work, where the PR practitioner seeks to influence media coverage, here PR people have direct control over their own – managed – media. Their messages can be promoted at will, while those seeking to put across alternative messages find these "media" closed to them. Thus internal communicators enjoy a monopoly of communication.

## Censorship

This monopoly also depends on the ability to censor rival forms of communication. Unlike other PR people, internal communicators enjoy the ability to apply real, formal sanctions. It is accepted – so much so that it usually passes without comment or consideration – that we relinquish many of our rights of free speech when we take up employment. The organizations which employ us are, with few exceptions, not democracies but autocracies or oligarchies. Individuals can be forced to imbibe ideas and information in all the ways described above, and at the same time they forfeit their right to speak out. Bringing one's employer into disrepute is a commonly accepted basis for dismissal, and breaching confidences and speaking to the media without permission often constitute disciplinary offences. The employer's monopoly of internal media leaves only informal channels of communication free. Typically these comprise emails and text messages, word of mouth exchanges – for example conversations around the water cooler or photocopier – or alternative forms of written media, such as graffiti.

This degree of control has been sharpened not just by the growth of increasingly professionalized internal communications regimes, but also by the teetering or collapse of alternative channels of communication, most notably those provided by trade unions. Of course astute internal communication experts realize that making their control too obvious is counterproductive. Sometimes limited dissent is allowed – staff comments are solicited – but this process is usually tokenistic and carefully circumscribed.

The BBC's staff newsletter, *Ariel*, has for years been nicknamed *Pravda* (the name of the former Soviet newspaper) by its intended audience, in recognition of its propagandistic qualities.

The resemblance between internal communication and propaganda does not stop there. Internal communication has the potential to deploy all the methods which have been used by propagandists down the ages, and typically uses a combination of overlapping approaches. Organizations do not have to rely on their own print or electronic media to put across their messages. They can augment them with a range of techniques which barely feature in conventional PR but are familiar to religious and political organizations.

In the words of the head of human resources at the mobile telephone company Orange, "I don't hold myself up to be a saint, but I try to incorporate the brand values into everything I do." Then he laughed. "It's beginning to sound like a cult."

Or as a Microsoft employee puts it, "People do say it's like the Moonies at Microsoft."[2]

Organizations control the physical environments in which people work and can use them to supplement their messaging. Even office lay-out – glass walls, open-plan, hot desking – conveys its own messages: these include openness, the importance of team playing, and a sense of urgency. Portraits and other works of art have always been used to illustrate the founding myths of institutions, and often their presence in the inner sanctums of power – corporate boardrooms for example – underlines their quasi-religious significance. Gradations of office furniture and decoration, as well as office size, can operate as incentive schemes, but the nature of design can be used to send subtle messages. Solid antique furniture and artworks can be used to reinforce a sense of tradition and inculcate a sense of timelessness, while more modern alternatives can do the reverse.

Internal communications strays further still. Even if there are no dress regulations, there may be informal but powerful pressures on what staff may wear and their outward appearance (indeed, it is noticeable that those who enjoy a notional freedom to choose their own clothing – for example in the "creative industries" – are often highly regimented in appearance). Induction processes and organizational programs of training blur unnoticeably into internal communication. Organizations can and do institute their own rituals and ceremonies both inside and outside formal working hours, including activities in leisure time which may involve families and members of local communities.

Internal communications is still in its infancy as a discipline. While all these and more techniques are employed, their use is seldom thoroughly planned and coordinated. One reason is that many internal communications techniques have emerged informally, over time. Another is that PR people seldom control all the levers of power. Human resources or personnel management still controls the internal communications function in some organizations, but even if PR is in formal charge of internal communications (and one major argument for this is that internal communications should merge seamlessly with external communications), in practice this does not mean that it fully controls it. Were it to do so the PR people would be the most powerful people in the organization, and – just as we have seen with propaganda – no chief executive or leader is likely to let that happen.

## The employer brand

A prevailing characteristic of internal communications is the desire to appear benign. Internal communications is traditionally seen as an extension of branding – it is sometimes called "employer branding" – and a way of enabling employees to act as ambassadors. It is also known as "change management," emphasizing the role it plays when organizations transform themselves, but despite this the way in which it comes to the fore when tougher messages have to be delivered is usually played down. The gap between employer concerns – maximum production at minimum cost – and employee concerns (typically job prospects and remuneration) is fudged, and the underlying message of "change management," change or leave, stays out of focus. Talk about internal communications is often imprecise and awash with euphemism, and any truth tends to be masked in a rosy glow. In cultures which value democracy and openness the iron hand of autocracy at the heart of corporate life has to be carefully wrapped in velvet and secretly made decisions have to appear to be the fruit of dialogue and consultation. The need for artifice and disingenuousness means it is no surprise that the writings and broadcasts of internal communicators have never been deemed to have any literary or artistic merit, unlike the best journalism.

Most articles about internal communications in Europe's leading PR trade magazine, *PR Week*, concern organizations which have to sack or redeploy large numbers of staff. Despite this the tone is usually comforting and unchallenging. There is one exception. A new managing director describes his first day:

"I arrived at 10am and at 11am I sacked the manufacturing director. At 12 noon I sacked the technical director, so by lunchtime everyone knew I had arrived."

The article draws the following conclusion:

"What makes this account so unsettling is that it explodes the warm and woolly thinking that can easily bedevil discussion of internal communication."

"To read half the articles on these topics you'd think that all a company had to do to be effective was empower people; have managers who give plenty of praise; create a listening culture and lo! the bottom line is magically transformed."[3]

The comforting nature of industry chatter about internal communications is helped along by a tendency to focus on sought-after workers with scarce skills in desirable jobs. But not all workers are difficult to recruit, or expensive to hire and train, and sometimes there may be a temptation to use internal communications in lieu of higher wages. The British supermarket chain Asda, owned by Walmart,

> admits it doesn't pay its 133,000 UK workforce particularly well – a basic £5.07 per hour – but it lavishes them with "Bursting with Pride" and "Thank You" certificates. There are "listening groups" and "huddles" and "colleagues circles" to hear their views and tell them about how the store is doing and to encourage a sense of "ownership."[4]

## Hidden persuaders

Internal communications has achieved another of the ultimate goals of the propagandist in the way in which it has crept up on contemporary employees without being noticed. The simple logic of propaganda is that in its ideal form it should do its work unobserved: it should not be ostensibly persuasive and should pass into people's minds without creating any friction. Internal communications largely achieves this. Although there is a cacophony of debate about modern marketing techniques, including advertising and PR, and their implications for society, internal communications is ignored. As we mentioned at the outset, it is so ubiquitous that that people do not notice it, while critics of the PR industry and scholars have surprisingly little to say about it.

Those who have internal communications – or something similar – in their job titles may not sound very frightening. Communication is after all seen as a positive thing. Nor, as we have seen, do they really control all forms of internal communication. But, taken together, the organs of internal communication are formidable, and, with increasingly professional planning and management, are today in a position to exert more control than ever. Like all PR, or propaganda, internal communications is not necessarily a bad thing, but it is not necessarily a good thing either. This is important because of the increasing role it plays in modern life. It affects all of us, not just in our working lives, but in education and beyond – indeed NGOs place particular emphasis on internal communications among their volunteers because they offer no pay. For most people in liberal democracies it is the closest they ever come to the powerful, closed propaganda systems associated with communism, fascism, or dystopian novels such as *1984* or *Brave New World*. But it carries on and grows, unchallenged, unexamined, and taken for granted. People who are truly interested in the role of PR in contemporary societies should pay it more attention.

"Trust, encouragement, reward, loyalty ... satisfaction. That's what I'm ... you know. Trust people and they'll be true to you. Treat them greatly, and they will show themselves to be great."

David Brent, *The Office*, BBC TV, Series 2, Episode 2

# CHAPTER 11

# PR and academia

## A degree of acceptance

It is quite possible that you know someone who has studied PR or is destined to do so. PR courses are sprouting in universities and colleges in many parts of the world. Once PR practitioners, if they had received any higher education at all, could have studied any subject. Anecdotal evidence suggests liberal arts disciplines were most common. Today, although PR graduates by no means have a stranglehold on the industry, increasing numbers of entrants have a PR qualification at undergraduate or postgraduate level. In most parts of the world this is a recent phenomenon, although the self-styled "Father of PR," Edward Bernays, taught PR in New York in the 1920s.[1] Some courses shun the term PR (the authors teach at the Sorbonne, where the term "relations publiques" were dropped some years ago as it sounded too superficial).

This might seem logical, given the popularity of PR as a career choice, the topicality of the subject matter (as only a glance at television and the newspapers shows), and the desire of universities, operating in a competitive marketplace of their own, to offer popular, *au courant* courses. However higher education has given PR courses only a hesitant welcome. Universities have been relatively slow to respond, and most of what are generally regarded as the world's leading universities do not deign to offer PR degrees, something that does not look like changing. (Indeed, when, late in life, Edward Bernays moved to Harvard with the hope that the University would be interested in his expertise, he was to be disappointed.[2])

Why might this be so? One reason is that PR has failed to find a secure home for itself amid the clusters of gated communities which constitute contemporary academia. Many people's first reaction might be to align PR alongside the study of mass communication or the media, given the common perception that PR is primarily about media relations. Some leading providers of mass communication and media courses do offer linked courses in PR (although it should be borne in mind that many of the world's best-known universities do not offer media-related courses).

However there will always be a feeling that PR people are cuckoos in the nest and that teaching people to practice PR is in some way unclean. After all, the study of mass communication is the heir to the Frankfurt School, those left-wing European thinkers and writers who fled the Nazi regime and its propaganda only to be horrified by the promotional culture they encountered in the United States. For people schooled in such a tradition journalism may at least have noble aims, even if they are imperfectly realized, and so the teaching of the practical skills of journalism generates less heartache for the intellectual descendants of those European émigrés than PR will ever do. Moreover journalists ensconced in universities often harbor their own trade's traditional antipathy to PR. (It is worth noting in passing that this blinkered attitude seems to be why so few journalism courses offer their students a proper introduction to PR. If you have an adversary it is surely far better to find out all you can about them.)

One might think that although a hostile view of PR might preclude universities from wanting to teach people how to practice PR, it might impel them to study the role and activities of the public relations industry. Surely a growing industry of this kind, however malevolent, should be closely monitored? However with few exceptions those who theorize about the media have been swifter to offer sweeping views of the PR industry than to engage in serious research. A cynic might say that such research might stand in the way of easy generalization: PR can remain a cartoon ogre.

There are other reasons why analyzing PR might seem hard as well as distasteful work. As a discipline PR offers few concrete products which can be readily held up for inspection, in the way that printed articles, broadcasts, or even advertisements can be. PR campaigns are nebulous things in which printed materials play only a part, and the skein of private emails, telephone calls, briefings, meetings and pseudo-events which constitutes so much of public relations is peculiarly difficult to unravel. As we have seen the most controversial aspects of PR work are seldom enshrined in press releases, nor would the archives of PR consultancies or in-house teams answer many critical questions. Indeed the workings of PR are often untraceable – or at least deniable. As we have discussed, PR is amorphous, operates under many aliases, and, as the industry has swollen, has become omnipresent. To try to keep tabs on the PR industry is to seek to study the façade of the contemporary world – an impossible, Herculean task.

In the absence of substantial documentation, PR researchers could rely on interviews, but these pose their own problems. If the best PR is indiscernible (as is frequently claimed) then what is the value of witness statements? Nor can the accounts of the actors themselves necessarily be taken at face value. Journalistic ideals mean that it is hard for journalists to admit that much of what they produce has been precooked by the PR industry. (It is noteworthy that when journalists rage about the impact of PR they always seem to refer to the work of other journalists, never their own!) Meanwhile, although the PR industry contains bumptious Bernays-like figures who cheerfully – and unreliably – lay claim to great feats of manipulation, there are many more PR practitioners who realize that claiming PR triumphs vitiates the very purpose of their work by undermining the third-party endorsement which they have labored to secure. This means that the key participants in the process of media production have a vested interest in denying what is happening. This not only creates insecure foundations for research, but leaves those teaching PR reliant on anecdotes and impressions to make their points.

## PR and business schools

As we have seen, many PR practitioners like to stress that their work is about far more than media relations. Indeed, as we have seen, and to use words which repeatedly recur in their speeches and writings, PR is a "strategic management tool," which should be prized by the chief executives of all organizations. For people who adopt this view, the proper place for the study of PR – perhaps under another title – is in a business school. Sadly their love for the world of business education is unrequited. Most leading business schools do not offer PR courses, and, in so far as they do, PR tends to find itself relegated to being a subset of the mighty discipline of marketing.

PR's lowly status at top business schools is in part a function of its role in the business world, discussed elsewhere. One of the problems we alluded to is that of evaluating PR. If money is the language of business, PR is inarticulate, because there are no commonly agreed techniques for measuring the success of PR activity, and none that enable PR people to show with much plausibility the financial benefits arising from their work. In real life PR's impact is assessed by personal judgment, but when it comes to business-oriented writing about PR there is often a vacuous feel to what is said. Textbooks are often long on uncritical claims, and laden with corporate language, but short of ascertainable facts and figures – a flabby foundation for teaching and learning. Not surprisingly one study showed that PR barely figured on MBA courses and came last on the rating of the most important elements for the career education of marketing professionals.[3]

## "Industry" approved degrees

Nor has the standing of PR as an academic discipline been helped by the attempt of elements within the PR industry to use the study of PR to bolster their flagging sense of self-esteem and remedy what they perceive as PR's damaged reputation. For example, the CIPR once stated that one of its key objectives, which it seeks to further in its work with universities and colleges (where it accredits many courses), is to "improve the standing of public relations as a strategic and rigorous management discipline."[4] The CIPR – and others – thus seek the endorsement of universities. Although this may be a sensible objective for a trade body which seeks to further its industry's goals, it sits unhappily with academia's ideals of free intellectual enquiry and independence. Although, it may be legitimate to theorize about how things should be, scholars have also to study the way things actually are and utter unpalatable truths. One significant justification for PR's place in academia is that that it is an important and growing industry which merits independent study in its own right. The critical views of colleagues in neighboring disciplines cannot all be simply pooh-poohed and dismissed. Crass attempts to raise the standing of PR in academia are doomed to failure: the more PR academics become obsessed with enhancing the reputation of PR the less seriously they will be taken as academics.

This problem extends beyond academia. Few observers, even those, like the authors, with ring-side seats, would say that that PR is an industry given to public reflection about its role in society. There are remarkably few introspective books or memoirs by senior PR people. The comparison with journalism, where there are countless examples of memoirs, is striking. Indeed one of the reasons that Edward Bernays was able to get so far with his paternity claim to the industry was that he remains one of very few practitioners to have bequeathed a full written record. There is an impasse: relatively few PR people have a formal training in the subject, and those that do have often been taught in a way which, as we saw above, seems intellectually dubious. This hardly equips them to secure the intellectual foundations of their industry. Such PR publications as exist are often characterized by rather desperate defensiveness as industry insiders mutter to each other about being misunderstood and being victims of unfair treatment. PR may have problems, they conclude, but things are always just about to improve for the better.

## Industry attitudes to PR degrees

If PR has difficulty sustaining itself within the ivory towers of academia, as a purely academic discipline, what about the role universities can play in nurturing the vocational skills of those who want to work in public relations? This has certainly been the mainstay of the existing provision of university teaching in PR, which after all depends on the large numbers of young people who want to enter the industry. While PR educators extol the virtues and relevance of their courses, the view of the PR industry has been more equivocal. Vested interests are at stake. The first PR consultants in many countries – and the industry is young enough for many of them to still be alive – were often not graduates themselves, and took some pride in their ability to create thriving careers for themselves without much formal education. They often had backgrounds which lay beyond PR – in journalism or advertising, for example – and could afford to be dismissive of new graduate entrants.

The second generation of PR people was more likely to have graduated, but their studies were seldom vocational. Before PR courses emerged, relatively few entrants to the PR industry had studied marketing or business studies, and very few had pursued postgraduate studies of any kind. It is this generation of PR practitioners which now makes most of the key decisions on recruitment and promotion within the industry. As graduates themselves they may have shed their predecessors' sometimes resentful attitude to university education, but by definition, through self-interest if nothing else, they tend to believe that experience of a high level of academic training is more important than the actual subject studied. They may also believe – but would be too polite to say – that their degrees are more worthwhile, and the institutions where they studied are more prestigious than those which offer PR courses.

Thus all sides in the debate about PR education bring prejudices to bear – students who invest time and money in PR courses presumably believe that they confer some advantages, while many employers believe that better established, more traditional courses have their advantages. There is certainly no evidence that graduates from other disciplines are hindered in their subsequent careers, despite their lack of subject-specific education. It is also worth pointing out that this particular debate is riddled with exceptions – enough to furnish anecdotal evidence for any point one wants to prove. There have been marketing graduates who have done well in PR – just as there have been graduates in every subject or none.

*   *   *

What practical conclusions is it possible to draw about the implications of this for an expanding and exceptionally diverse industry? Emerging from a well-known university is always going to carry a cache – in the PR industry as well as in other walks of life – and there is little sign of many sought-after universities relenting in their opposition to PR degrees. However all is not necessarily lost for PR graduates: their acquisition of practical skills, knowledge of the industry, opportunities for networking, and evidence of a commitment to a career in PR may redress the balance in their favor at entry level, helping them to get started. The demonstration of commitment is of particular importance because, while many occupations which require prolonged prior training can reasonably assume that relatively few recruits will abandon their jobs for different careers, things are different in PR, where many recruits enter on a whim. The advantage all of this gives PR graduates may then wither away, but sometimes getting through the door is enough. Finally, as more and more PR graduates join and rise up the industry, the old prejudices are likely to decline and the chances of a recent graduate in PR being interviewed by an old graduate in PR will increase.

While determination and the acquisition of practical skills may often be sufficient to join PR's foot soldiery, progression in the PR industry depends on skills which are harder to inculcate at a university. We have argued that the best PR people are dilettantes, a notion that many in the industry strenuously resist (at least in public) because it seems unflattering. However the essence of PR is surface-skimming – dipping in and out of different subjects quickly, simplifying the often complicated issues involved, and then communicating the desired messages to the intended audiences.

## Where are the text books?

The lack of truly authoritative textbooks undermines PR's standing in higher education just as much as its claims to professional status. A fledgling discipline can hardly hold its head up without a battery of serious literature, but those PR textbooks which do exist are hardly required reading. Despite protestations to the contrary there is little evidence that a growing and thriving PR industry makes use of textbooks to develop its skills. It is hard to prove a negative, particularly when people naturally wish to pay lip service to learning, but we know that the offices of leading PR practitioners are usually all but devoid of PR books. Specialist business directories, books by management gurus, and occasionally studies of marketing may lurk on shelves, but seldom books on PR *per se*. To back up this anecdotal evidence we conducted a survey of one of the world's largest PR consultancies. Most respondents claimed to have read books on PR – but most could not remember what the books were: it is reasonable to assume that the books did not have a great influence. Of the handful who could remember what they had read, several of the titles mentioned were in fact more general works on business, management, or marketing.

Despite occasional bluster to the contrary, the PR industry makes little use of academic research – and it certainly would if it could secure competitive advantage by so doing. Although the pioneers of PR such as Bernays and Ivy Lee made much of the then new discipline of psychology, PR offices are hardly bedecked with the fruits of university research, nor do they compete for research students – in fact the links between industry and research (such as there is) are weak.

This situation reflects the reality that, in the main, PR people learn by doing, and so hopefully doing it better, than through study. Textbooks can play a role, but there will always be a problem about studying to be creative. As we have seen, many are attracted to PR because of its creativity, and the rigid rules which apply in, say, law or accountancy do not apply. Moreover, because securing third-party endorsement lies at the heart of PR, the discipline cannot be replicated in the classroom as readily as other media-related disciplines. Student journalists can research and produce unpublished and unbroadcast material that, at its best, might be of the same quality as that which appears in the media. Would-be advertisers can also create unused advertising material. But no-one can create an unused PR campaign, because PR is an interactive, communicative process where control of the product is relinquished to others (most commonly journalists) before it makes its final appearance.

While students can present ideas for PR campaigns and prepare all kinds of PR-related materials, they cannot deal with journalists or engage with audiences on a realistic basis in the classroom, and the variables to which PR activity is subject cannot be fully replicated. Mock-ups and simulated exercises can be attempted, and work experience and real-life projects can help to bridge the void, but it is difficult for PR educators fully to imitate the brutal realities that PR people have to confront.

**Blog comment**

What really counts are the core skills – writing, media relations, cleint liaison – enthusiasm, contiual improvement, ability to play office politics, hard work, tenacity and luck. [sic]

Posted by: rob baker November 01, 2006
at 08:19 a.m.[5]

# CHAPTER 12

# Lobbying, public affairs, politics, and government PR

## Paying for influence

Lobbyists are important creatures of our age. Their activities are seldom long out of the news in the United States and the United Kingdom, and scandals involving lobbying infect most democracies from time to time. The word is often used in the same breath as PR, so there is plenty of guilt by association. As with PR, and as the title of this section reveals, this has led to some awkwardness about what to call the "lobbying." Although it may be the term in general use by lay-people, and the one, crucially, that is used in the media, in the United Kingdom practitioners seldom call themselves lobbyists. Many opt for "public affairs," which is often the term preferred by the big international consultancies, although those who work in the not-for-profit sector tend to dodge all these terms (just as they avoid calling what they do PR) and lump their activities together as campaigning.

Lobbying (or public affairs) may be defined as any activity designed to influence the actions of those who exercise the powers of government. This includes not just national governments, but all places where political power is located and wherever decisions are made on laws and regulations and their implementation. Beyond national legislatures lobbying embraces central government ministries, agencies, and a growing army of regulators. It includes regional and local tiers of government, but it also covers an ever-spreading array of international organizations, operating either globally – for example the United Nations, the International Monetary Fund, the

World Trade Organization – or in different parts of the world – for example ASEAN (the Association of Southeast Asian Nations), NAFTA (the North American Free Trade Area), the European Union, and the African Union.

Rather like PR itself, activity of this kind is timeless – the techniques may vary, but it has been attempted in all societies throughout history. Businesses and others have always had an interest in influencing government decisions: what is new is that they now do so in a planned and deliberate way, using specialist staff. However the origins of the term "lobbying" itself are telling. They derive from the lobby of the Willard Hotel in Washington DC where businessmen and others sought to waylay the US President Grant (President 1869–1877).[1] Since then lobbying has become a large, specialized discipline in its own right, employing tens of thousands of people in Washington alone. The biggest center outside North America is in Brussels, the hub of the European Union's administration.

In the United States and Europe lobbying gradually assumed its modern form as the role of governments in society and economic life grew. However the market liberalization which began in the 1980s and which continues to sweep the world has given lobbying an enormous boost. Large parts of the economy which were in state hands are now privately owned and administered: direct government control may have ended, but government legislation and regulation have an enormous impact on how businesses are run, and hence businesspeople want to influence such decisions. Increasingly governments respond to popular anxieties about issues – be they to do with security, food, medical treatment, health and safety, environmental or other matters – through legislation and regulation. Governments also have to grapple with the consequences of increasingly rapid change: new phenomena such as the World Wide Web can sweep the world at an unprecedented speed, and as governments take urgent measures to seek to control or regulate such developments, those outside government resort to lobbying to protect their interests.

Research we undertook for our book *Public Relations for Asia* pointed to the likelihood of strong growth in public affairs work in Asia. Not only does the growth of lobbying formalize more traditional methods of seeking to influence government in ways that meet the needs of a modern market economy and which can be used by multinational companies, but in countries such as China a continuing legacy of strong government control places a particular premium on lobbying.

The work of lobbyists can be broken down as follows:

- First, and most minimally, to provide information and advance warning. In the modern world it is hard for any organization to keep up with the large amounts of legislation and regulation which might affect it (and which may have serious cost implications). Even if it is impossible to influence government, the more advance notice organizations have the more they are able to prepare themselves. Thus many organizations pay lobbyists to monitor the work of obscure arms of government, legislatures, and international organizations – and indeed even some government organizations pay for such services in order to find out about what the rest of government is up to, so big and so complex has the work of government become.

- To amend proposed government or legislative measures, to stop them in their tracks or, if all else fails, to overturn them. This is the classic focus of lobbying. Lobbyists always urge the need to get involved at the earliest stage in the policy-making process, before policy is settled. The earlier they are involved, the easier it is to change policy. However lobbying can continue up to and beyond the passage of legislation and the taking of formal decisions (there is, for example, often considerable leeway about the way new laws are implemented).

- Lobbying can also be used to advocate government action – a classic focus of NGO activity.

As with other forms of PR, lobbying can be undertaken "in-house," by lobbyists who are directly employed by the organization, or by an external lobbying firm – or by a combination of the two. Only relatively large organizations or ones which are particularly concerned about government action will normally deem it worthwhile to employ full time lobbyists, but many businesses are members of trade organizations and one of the main functions of such bodies is to lobby on behalf of the common interests of their members. Some organizations will retain the services of lobbying firms to keep a watching brief and then use them for specific campaigns when the need arises.

Like PR people generally, lobbyists can come from a range of backgrounds: no specific qualifications are required. However, just as journalistic expertise is often valued in mainstream PR, political and governmental experience is often an entry ticket to the world of lobbying. In order to influence government, a proper understanding of the way it works is essential, and direct personal knowledge of key personalities is seen as advantageous.

## Lobbying's links to PR

Some lobbyists like to distance themselves from the PR industry. They see media relations work as a blunt instrument compared with their ability to target the real decision-makers in government. This reflects the fact that effective lobbying often involves contact with only a handful of carefully chosen people, rather than the larger audiences PR typically seeks to influence. Such lobbyists are likely to be employed by independent, specialist lobbying firms which do not undertake general PR work. However almost all large PR consultancies offer lobbying as part of their menu of services and therefore employ specialist staff: it is now part of what clients expect. While lobbying can be carried on discreetly and effectively, lobbying campaigns may be combined with other PR activity in pursuit of common objectives. This reflects the fact that all political organizations pay great heed to media coverage and public opinion, and so PR can be used to apply additional pressure. The vital connection between PR and lobbying is demonstrated by the way in which many companies want the lobbying and PR services which they buy to come under the same roof – even though they have historically been content to buy their PR and advertising from different suppliers.

## Lobbying issues

Asked about a glamorous party funding event held by President Bush Senior, his spokesman, Marlin Fitzwater, replied:

"It's buying access to the system, yes. That's what the political parties and the political operation is all about." ... Asked how other, less wealthy citizens could buy into the system, Mr Fitzwater said, "They have to demand access in other ways."[2]

Two major, interlinked issues haunt any discussion of lobbying. The first is that the ability of the rich and powerful to pay for the skills of lobbyists is unfair and gives such people and organizations a stronger voice in society's decision-making process. The second is the hardy perennial of corruption. Lobbying in many societies has been connected with political fundraising scandals and even the personal enrichment of politicians and officials. The stigma attached to lobbying is one of the main reasons that "lobbyists" seek to use other terms to describe what they do.

The first issue is a little more nuanced than it might appear. Critics of lobbying tend to highlight the role played by wealthy businesses, and it is true that most of the clients of lobbying firms are large firms pursuing their interests. However nongovernmental organizations or NGOs are themselves adept users of lobbying techniques, even though they distance themselves from the term. As we have seen, campaigning is a core business for NGOs, and NGO leaders gain experience of lobbying and PR throughout their careers, and are often promoted on the strength of their abilities in these arenas. In contrast business leaders often emerge because of their mastery of a narrower range of technical and financial skills, and usually lack the PR aptitude and experience of the NGO leadership (the exceptional business leaders we have all heard of, people with charisma and high profiles, tend to be just that: the exceptions). As far back as the 1950s Irwin Ross made the point that American trade unions – in many ways the precursors of today's not-for-profit campaigning organizations – did not need to spend as much on PR as businesses did: trade union leaders were familiar with PR techniques in ways which few business leaders could rival.[3]

Hostility to corporate interests can also blind critics to the fact that the business world is itself far from monolithic. Big businesses are in competition with each other, and different business sectors are also in competition. Smaller businesses which are unable to afford to do their own lobbying are frequently represented by trade associations. So governments tend to hear from a range of commercial interests, alongside not-for-profit organizations, before they make decisions. The extent to which governments are influenced by these competing voices is all but impossible to assess. Governments may be happy to be seen as listening to different points of view as that is seen as positive, but are reluctant to be seen as acting under pressure, and so are not wholly reliable when it comes to admitting the degree to which lobbyists shape their decisions. On the other hand, like PR (and advertising) people, lobbyists both overclaim and underclaim: when they are seeking business it is in their interests to talk up their successes; but when they or their industry face criticism it is in their interests to play down their role.

Those who speak up for lobbying would argue that it is not only an inevitable part of life but a necessary and positive one. It is a modern, professionalized embodiment of the ancient right of people to petition their rulers, and, by extension, to seek the advice and support of others to help them do so. Modern governments are responsible for a vast array of policy areas, and this involves drafting and implementing detailed and intricate laws and regulations. They cannot hope to keep abreast of all the information and opinions they need on their own. Lobbying is a means of providing them with the raw material required to make informed decisions which reflect the different interests in their societies.

Even the sternest critics of lobbying are left floundering when it comes to devising practical policies for regulating the activities of lobbyists, although that does not mean there have been many attempts. When the office of Mayor of London was established the first incumbent, Ken Livingstone, announced that he was going to exclude all lobbyists from the new Greater London Authority building, but this ran into the sand.[4] The impracticalities of regulating lobbying abound. Many lobbyists work in-house and have a range of job titles. They often work closely with colleagues who are not involved in lobbying, and indeed lobbyists often say that it is better for them to take a back seat when it comes to meetings and direct involvement with government. The only watertight way to ensure there was no contact between in-house lobbyists and government would be to prohibit any contact with external organizations – and even if this were possible the prevention would surely be worse than the disease. Not only would government be denied the oxygen of outside information and opinion, but the fundamental right to petition government, enshrined, for the Anglo-Saxon world, in Magna Carta, would be threatened.

It might seem easier to envisage the regulation of lobbying activity by stand-alone lobbying firms or PR consultancies which also offer lobbying services, but even then there are problems. The first is the definitional problem. As noted, such firms may shy away from the term lobbying and use a range of other terms. It is also hard to come up with a watertight definition of lobbying. As we have seen, PR and lobbying activity can blur together. A law firm may help its clients lobby, and indeed some have set up specialist lobbying arms for this purpose. This could easily apply across the professional services sector. In short, lobbying is so timeless and fundamental an activity that clumsy regulation or proscription will just displace it or lead it to adopt a disguise.

The cloudiness of definition overlaps with the instinctive prejudices of many critics of lobbying. For them the bugbear is corporate lobbying: the activities of NGOs and campaigning organizations, which normally conduct their lobbying work in-house, and which are usually more focused on lobbying than commercial organizations can allow themselves to be, are not scrutinized because the critics are fundamentally in sympathy with the campaigners' objectives and do not even categorize their work as "lobbying."

These problems are compounded by a characteristic which lobbying shares with PR: so much activity, including the most contentious aspects of it, takes place privately, in the course of small meetings and one-to-one conversations. This means that what takes place is one person's word against another's. Attempts can be made to register meetings with lobbyists, but, as we have seen, lobbyists may deliberately choose to remain in the background, simply helping to prepare for and arrange such meetings.

## Lobbying regulation

Like PR, lobbying's propagandists often see their trade heading toward the sunny uplands of moral probity, leaving any dubious associations far behind. Of course there is no reason why lobbyists should be more or less ethical than anyone else. Much lobbying is routine, mundane, and rather inconsequential. However lobbying scandals keep resurfacing around the world, leading to calls for action to curb particular forms of activity. No sooner has one set of rules been imposed than another breach occurs. There will always be those who bend or break the rules. Lobbyists often assert publicly that it is their understanding of the processes of government that really matters, not personal connections, but there is compelling evidence that when they feel it is to their advantage, especially when they seek new business, they boast about the people they know and the way they can achieve access to decision-makers.

"There are 17 people who count. And to say I am intimate with every one of them is the understatement of the century."
Former British lobbyist and Labour Party insider Derek Draper[5]

Inevitably some politicians and decision-makers will be corrupt – no system of regulation or policing can wholly rule this out – and it follows that some lobbyists will always be tempted to exploit this weakness on the basis that it will not be uncovered. It is not always as blatant as the "cash for parliamentary questions" affair in 1990s Britain, or the Abramoff scandal in Washington. Where does legitimate hospitality end and treating begin? Is finger food okay, but a sit down meal too much? Can skilful operators influence politicians as much by the prospect of gifts or future employment as by gifts themselves?

A bigger systemic problem in contemporary democracies arises from political parties' need to attract funding from wealthy individuals and companies in order to finance the costs of running their election campaigns. Even if there are no strings attached to the money given, there will always be suspicions surrounding donations from people whose businesses are affected by a plethora of government decisions. Providing funds to political parties all but guarantees access to senior politicians – dinners, receptions, and so on are the staples of fundraising. Proving cause and effect between donation and decision is usually impossible, as the process is normally veiled and subtle, often involving many tiers of intermediaries. And politicians would not be human if, as they banked current donations, they did not consider how their behavior might affect future largesse. The appearance of favors being given, however hotly denied, always risks dragging lobbyists and politicians into disrepute.

## Politics and spin

Most business leaders may be uncomfortable communicators, but the politicians who govern us have always embraced the arts of communication. PR skills loom large in a politician's armory. Even dictatorships care about public opinion, but in democracies it is the lifeblood of politics, just as financial realities and the iron laws of supply and demand constitute the foundation for business activity.

This makes it hard to disentangle PR from government. Politicians' sensitivity to public opinion has meant that in many countries they have distanced themselves from the term public relations as it has acquired negative overtones, often preferring words such as "Information" or the hard-to-disapprove-of "Communication." But the vital connection between PR and politics can be traced back to the origins of the industry, when many of its founders honed their skills galvanizing support for the United States intervention in the First World War. As reaching vast audiences via the mass media replaced public speaking and debating as the prime means of political communication, modern PR skills have become ever more central.

**Politicians and PR**

Ronald Reagan's progression from screen acting to politics and the US Presidency included many years working in public relations for big business in the United States.

In France the largest PR consultancy, I&E, was founded by Coup de Frejac, formerly Charles de Gaulle's ADC during the Second World War.

The head of the UK's largest PR consultancy, Lord Tim Bell, started in advertising but earned his PR spurs working for Margaret Thatcher. Although his PR consultancies do a wide range of commercial work, they are also involved in political and governmental work in the United Kingdom and overseas.

Mark Penn worked on the Hilary Clinton campaign in 2007/2008 while also running PSB, part of the PR giant Burson-Marsteller.

It is in the United Kingdom that PR is achieving its political apotheosis. The current challenger for the premiership, the Conservative Party leader David Cameron, has a PR background, while the present Prime Minister, Gordon Brown, is married to a well-known PR woman (and both his brothers work in PR).

If the world of politics avoids using the term public relations to describe its communications work, then so do outside commentators and members of the public. In the Anglo-Saxon world the word that has emerged to describe political communications work is *spin*. The people who perform this role are spin doctors. The nickname is of US origin. Its use can be traced back to 1977 and seems to originate in baseball. It is derived from the way in which the pitcher can manipulate the ball as he throws it towards the catcher, thereby tricking the batter (the fact that this is analogous to the use of spin in cricket helped make the term readily understood in other English-speaking, cricket playing, countries).[6]

As a pejorative term for political communication spin came into vogue in the United Kingdom in the 1990s, and was firmly associated with New Labour, the then party leader Tony Blair, and the project to revitalize the party through improved communications and thereby wrest back power from the Conservatives.

Spin is firmly associated with the exercise of power – when employed beyond politics the term tends to refer to high-level corporate maneuvering, not day-to-day marketing PR. It conveys, more powerfully than the term PR itself, a sense of manipulation and even sinister menace. As we have seen, its senior practitioners, in fact and fiction, are more likely to be male than female, a reversal of the world of commercial PR which is largely populated by women or "PR girls." Governments may prefer to talk about communication and information: spin implies that the information communicated is carefully selected and delivered in a way that is to the advantage of the sender of the message. Since so much is at stake, the methods used can be ruthless, and telling the truth may not be a priority. The term's omnipresence in contemporary Anglo-Saxon culture is surely because it so aptly captures all the nuances that are inherent to the world of political communication.

References to spin can be found well beyond the news media: now no representation of political life is complete without a sinister and overweeningly powerful spin doctor. When the British television series *Yes Minister* and *Yes Prime Minister* were first aired on the BBC in the 1980s, these acclaimed satires of contemporary political life contained only occasional and minor roles for a press secretary. The politicians were concerned about media handling, as were their officials, but it was only one of their preoccupations. Today, from *Spin City* and *The West Wing* to the BBC's *The Thick of It* and *Absolute Power*, spin doctors abound. The unstated thinking is that no depiction of modern politics could ring true without them.

## Why political PR is different

Spin may not be unique to politics, but it exemplifies the way in which media relations is central to politics. It is a two-way street, for politics is central to the media in a way that companies are not. Only a company going through a major crisis begins to get the kind of sustained media coverage that governments routinely receive. Presidents and prime ministers feature on the front pages or at the head of news bulletins in a way that would make most corporate chief executives blanch – and rightly so, because such coverage might well indicate that their jobs were on the line. The media relations aspects of PR work are also particularly important for another reason. In many societies – including the United Kingdom – political advertising is banned or sharply curtailed, forcing politicians to rely on editorial content to promote themselves and their policies.

Political marketing takes place in a different context to its commercial counterpart, which is why glib and lazy comparisons have to be qualified. The principle behind commercial PR is that its practitioners are informing people who exercise individual choices (and, then, usually, enjoy rights to seek redress if they have legitimate grounds for dissatisfaction with their choice). In the political realm the options are much more limited. The choice normally arises once every few years, and involves a decision which forces people to choose one supplier for all their political needs, without any rights of redress or money-back guarantees. Above all it is a collective "choice": the government has full powers to govern and those who oppose it are subject to its authority as it compels its citizens to act in various ways. This means that often the language of the commercial world does not ring true in the world of government. All of this forms the backdrop to a number of further differences between political PR and its commercial counterpart:

- Companies, however large and complex, are simpler organisms than modern democratic governments. Within the law, their obligation is to do whatever best serves the interests of the people who own them, their shareholders. Democratic governments have a split agenda. On the one hand they are controlled by political parties which are forever campaigning for reelection, but on the other hand they have responsibilities to all citizens, and beyond that to the international community. To put it simply, if you and a company choose to have nothing to do with each other that is normally – unless monopoly conditions apply – the end of the matter. Not so with government: you may abhor the governing party but you still have to pay your taxes, and on the other hand you are entitled to the state's protection and whatever services it provides. This has considerable ramifications for communication. Commercial organizations can choose to ignore audiences: for example, if you are unlikely either to be a potential customer, or to influence one, then communicating with you about products is a waste of resources. The political parties which control democratic governments have to try to suppress this instinct. Diehard opponents have to be told about state services and communicated with on the same basis as existing and potential supporters. This cleavage between governmental responsibility (providing essential information) and political marketing aspirations (showing how good you are in the hope of being reelected) is at the heart of much of the debate about government communication.

- Access to taxpayer funding means that Governments have potentially unlimited resources for communication at their disposal. In addition to employing thousands of their own PR staff they can hire PR consultancies and can also engage in associated activity such as advertising. No company can match this scale of activity. Large-scale and sophisticated communication is necessary if governments are to inform their citizenry about what they are doing, but given the dichotomy described above there will always be a temptation to exploit this advantage in the hope of getting reelected rather than helping citizens. To some extent this advantage can be seen as part of the legitimate spoils of electoral victory, but perhaps the real reason this in-built advantage is not subject to more than sporadic scrutiny is that opposition parties and politicians look forward to using it themselves when the political wheel of fortune turns in their favor.

- However, not everything favors governments. Whereas businesses face competition from other companies which are in engaged in similar day-to-day activities, in democratic politics the position is different. Opposition parties are not responsible for anything (apart from the limited but important matter of running their own campaign machines). Instead they are campaigning organizations which enjoy great freedom to choose what they wish to speak about and propose. But governments are responsible for an enormous range of functions. Their PR people have to defend a long border. Not only may the opposition attack at any point, but governments are constantly at the mercy of events. Whether it is 9/11, Hurricane Katrina, or the administrative bungles or party funding scandals which have beset the Labour Government in the United Kingdom, at any time government may be put on the defensive about an unexpected problem, at home or abroad.

- As mentioned, the targets of companies' PR activities are ultimately a matter of commercial judgment. This means that the wealthier and more powerful you are, the more likely it is commercial PR people will try to influence you: you are, for example, more likely to buy more of the goods and services their paymasters produce, or to own or buy shares. Poor, powerless people are of less interest. Here government and political PR march to two different tunes. Government PR turns the commercial model inside out by being (or affecting to be) *more* interested in the weak and poor: government benefits and services are often designed with precisely such people in mind. Whereas the wealthy and powerful are frequently regarded as able to look after their own interests, their counterparts are the intended audiences for advice on such matters as financial benefits, health, education, training, employment, and housing. The political position is different. The brutal realities of political campaigning mean that the only target audience that matters comprises people who: (1) are likely to vote (so increasingly the elderly matter more than young people as they are more likely to cast votes); (2) might vote for the party concerned, but might not (committed voters are unlikely to be swayed); and (3) vote where their votes count (this will depend on the electoral system, but piling up surplus majorities in particular areas achieves nothing). If they are likely to vote for a rival party, the logic is that it is better to discourage them from voting at all.

- In commercial marketing market share matters, but market size is all-important. There is little point in a company increasing its market share if its sales plunge. In politics market share is king: there is no point in winning a record vote if your opponent does even better, and conversely a victory on a low turn-out is still a victory.

- Political PR is much more likely to be negative than its commercial counterpart. Commercial PR realizes that negative campaigns raise awareness of rival companies, making potential customers more likely to consider alternative options. It is significant that the best-known negative commercial campaigns involve competition between well-known rival brands, where the danger of raising awareness can be set to one side. Such campaigns, which can degenerate into mudslinging, can seem undignified. They risk putting off those they seek to influence and dragging the entire sector into disrepute. In politics the stakes are different, for the winner normally takes all, and negative campaigning is carried on with few holds barred. In most democratic elections there are only two realistic contenders. Both are high-profile, so the dangers of publicizing a rival can be largely ignored. And, in their anxiety to win power through the ballot box, the other pitfalls of negative campaigning are overlooked. Students of politics might like to consider the effect on the public image of politicians and political life as a whole. How would we change our view of a business sector if its leaders publicly tore into each other in the way we have come to expect of politicians?

- The reliance on negative campaigning is inseparable from the way in which political marketing is personality based – to a much greater extent than its commercial equivalent. While some chief executives have become well known, most people do not associate individual names and faces with most of the products they buy. Instead companies rely on the public choosing brands that they make identifiable through PR, advertising, and other forms of marketing. In politics the position is reversed. Politicians may try to create branded products – new political initiatives and programs – but in most cases the branding is weak. Relatively few resonate down the years, and even those which do – such as the New Deal or the National Health Service – struggle to compete with the prominence of political leaders from those times, such as President Roosevelt or Winston Churchill. Individual politicians, their lives, and even the lives of their families, are the focus of media coverage in a way which is rarely equaled in the world of business, not least because the media like to tell stories based on personalities rather than abstract policies. This focus is reflected in political PR.

- The reliance on personality is partly a consequence of the use of modern marketing techniques in politics. In mature markets there is seldom much difference between competing products – the drive for competitive advantage means that most distinguishing features of successful products are ironed out quickly as competitors emulate them. Blind tasting may reveal that most people cannot tell the difference between the best-selling lagers, or prefer Pepsi to its better-selling rival, but a massive investment in marketing ensures that people are not only aware of the separate brands but express brand preferences. A similar process has occurred in politics. Political parties such as the UK Labour Party, which were once driven by ideologies and by policies determined by party activists, found that its traditional approach did not provide effective platforms for winning elections. Increasingly sophisticated market research techniques are now used to find out what people want, and then politicians seek to sell themselves as the people who can deliver it. The logical consequence of this – since all parties use similar market research techniques – is that parties offer very similar policies (although because they are in competition, this is something they fiercely deny). If policies do not elicit support, they are quickly modified or dropped. What then distinguishes political parties and candidates? Beyond a lingering afterglow from the ideological past, the main, irreducible, difference is personality. While PR and other techniques can have some impact on how a personality is perceived, an individual's unique personality is not something that can be readily changed. It is tempting to see personality playing an ever-greater role in contemporary elections – a trend which is compounded by the media's natural interest in personality based stories.

# CHAPTER 13

# Does PR work and is it good for us?

> He operates in a no-man's land between advertisement and argument.
>
> Malcolm Muggeridge, British journalist, on the PR practitioner.[1]

Society demonstrably wants PR. More and more money is being spent on PR services. Businesses and politicians, charities, NGOs, educational organizations, and even churches and other religious bodies – all pour resources into PR. But does PR always work and is it always good for us? There are plenty of critics who see PR as a negative force in society: distorting markets, privileging the rich and powerful, encouraging mindless consumerism, and promoting a celebrity-fixated dumbing down of culture. Having earlier examined the political impact of PR, this chapter looks at the effectiveness and impact of PR in the economic and social fields.

## PR and economics

Critics may portray PR as smug and all-powerful, but it faces its own problems. One of the biggest is evaluation. How much was a particular success or failure down to PR and how much due to other marketing or marketing communication techniques? Did wider social or economic trends play a role? Even if it can be shown that PR played a role it is hard to demonstrate that it offered value for money. Is one PR campaign for something simply canceled out by a rival PR campaign against it? Not only are these difficult questions, but the evaluation needed to answer them is generally expensive and difficult to do.

Many of the entries in PR award schemes claim effectiveness, but normally all they can prove is that they have successfully obtained coverage in the media. While research evidence from Hill & Knowlton and Yankelovich claims that 34% of public opinion is shaped by media coverage (in comparison to 4% for advertising) this does not constitute proof for every PR campaign.[2] There are examples where the media seem to have little if any impact on public attitudes or behavior. For instance, the Danish electorate voted overwhelmingly against joining the European currency despite the fact that 46 out of 48 media outlets supported the move as did government and business.[3] Artists, writers, and actors are all familiar with works that are critically acclaimed by the media but bomb commercially. Similarly there are products, programs, and people that are reviled in the media and enjoy enormous commercial success. Newspaper editors and TV, radio, and online journalists all over the world are familiar with the fickleness of the public who fail to become excited and involved in the media's latest campaign.

Some PR theorists such as Alison Theaker concur with media scholars that, while the media is good at setting the agenda of what people think about,[4] it is less effective at influencing their actual thoughts. Moreover, only 36% of the public, according to research by *USA Today*/CNN/Gallup Polls, believe what the media tell them.[5] This is a serious issue for an industry that earns so much of its money from its proclaimed ability to influence the media and to manage, if not control, content. The problem is not confined to traditional media. For all the hype about online and digital forums most of the infinite amounts of cyber-space commentary appears to have little or no impact, notwithstanding a few – oft-quoted – exceptions. (It is also notable that advocates for the importance of digital coverage proclaim its success most loudly when digital coverage and commentary is picked up in "mainstream" media.)

So if the media is less influential than was thought, or than it used to be, what is the future for PR?

In spite of, or perhaps because of, these issues organizations continue to invest in the booming media evaluation industry. AMEC (The Association for the Measurement and Evaluation of Communication) now has 29 members around the world who earn over £40 million in evaluation revenues, although to put this in perspective this is less than 4% of the total revenue claimed for the UK PR consultancy industry alone. AMEC's members may adopt slightly different techniques as they analyze media coverage for their clients, but there are three main ways of evaluating or measuring results. These are *output, outtake*, and *outcome*.

## Output

Output is the most common way of measuring PR results, though also the least meaningful. Output means media coverage that results from, or is the output of, planned PR activity.

Output can be measured in a variety of ways. The most basic is *circulation (reach)*. This means the number of people who could have seen or heard the planned messages. It is a rather coarse measure as it fails to take account of whether the coverage is good, bad, or indifferent. Nor does it gauge whether people took on board the messages or changed their behavior. More sophisticated measures of output attempt to ascertain the inclusion of key messages, the favorability of the coverage and the extent to which the target audience has been penetrated. These measures are of interest, particularly when compared with the performance of competitors, but they do not prove effectiveness – unless of course the original objective was simply to secure press coverage.

The advantages of measuring by output are that is it is relatively cheap, easy to do, and readily understood. The disadvantages are that it fails to tell anyone what the PR actually achieved in terms of attitudinal or behavioral changes. It only tells you if you have had good press coverage. To find out if attitudes have changed practitioners have to look at "outtake."

## Outtake

Outtake measures people's changes in attitude after they have heard or read a PR message, but not whether they alter their behavior. For example, do people now believe, as had been planned, that company x is a superior manufacturer? Have they changed their mind about a proposal to build a new factory? Are they willing to consider a different brand next time they make a purchase?

The only way of finding this out is through research. If, for example, 50% of a research sample say they have been influenced in the way desired by those orchestrating the PR then it is not unreasonable to conclude that 50% of all those exposed to the messages were influenced in the same way. Not unreasonable, but not proof.

The advantage of this approach is that it gives a clearer indication of whether the messages have got through. However, it is not cheap. Indeed a true measure of what a PR campaign has achieved normally requires a preliminary benchmarking survey to find out what people thought before the campaign and later research to test its effects. Such research is often out of reach for smaller companies, and fails the cost-benefit test for all but large PR campaigns. Moreover, this sort of research can never be totally accurate: it only looks at a sample, not the whole target audience; and people are not totally honest when answering researcher's questions.

Answers relating to sex, money, and morality are notoriously fickle. Even when answering a computer-based questionnaire people like to look good. Admitting you are promiscuous, mean, or immoral does not generally enhance people's self-esteem so they tend to be less honest than they might think. If people were really as green or "ethical" about their purchases as they claim in surveys, product sectors such as organic food, low energy light bulbs, and fair-trade cotton would be very big business indeed. Moreover PR does not take place in a vacuum: people are influenced by other factors such as advertising or wider social trends, but it is hard to pin down the relative weight of the different influences. It is also the case that by asking people questions you are obliging them to take an interest in something that may not really concern them: surveys have great difficultly in establishing how strongly people feel about an issue.

Edward Bernays' "Torches of Liberty" stunt in 1929 was one of the most celebrated PR events of the twentieth century. It was designed to make cigarette smoking acceptable to women and features in many books and TV histories of PR.[6]

Bernays persuaded a number of New York debutantes to conceal cigarettes while taking part in the city's Easter Day parade. At a given moment they all lit up. Newspaper photographers had been alerted and the event received extensive press coverage.

In most accounts Bernays' work is accepted uncritically as a brilliant PR stunt and a triumph of the persuasive arts. The story is an appealing one which was skillfully promoted by Bernays himself. So anxious are people to see Bernays as a master-manipulator that they seldom pause for thought. But in fact smoking among women was on the rise well before Bernays' campaign. Social factors – including the emancipation of women and increased female employment outside the home – as well as extensive advertising, all played their part. Bernays probably contributed to a process which was already underway but his exact role can never be quantified. It was almost certainly much less significant than he is given credit for: the greatest achievement of the Torches of Liberty event was to secure everlasting PR for Bernays himself. Rather ironically, it is critical media treatments such as the BBC TV series *Century of the Self* in 2002 that have been in large part responsible for perpetuating the Bernays myth.

## *Outcome*

The most effective way of measuring a PR campaign is to look at changes in behavior, or outcome: the final effects of your activity. The measurement of outcome is comparatively easy when PR is the only communication discipline in use and there are no other factors. Any increase in sales, calls to the help center, hits on the website, changes in voting intentions, and so forth, can be simply be put down to the PR campaign. Proof perfect that the PR has worked. You can even work out the cost per sale, enquiry, or vote by dividing the cost of the PR campaign by the total response figure. However in practice there are normally other communication disciplines or other circumstances which have an important bearing on the outcome.

\* \* \*

Perhaps the only certainty is that the evaluation of Public Relations campaigns is fraught with problems, and yet without proper evaluation of its effectiveness PR cannot claim to be a measurable management discipline like its established counterparts. The proper evaluation of PR results remains something more talked about than practiced, even at the highest levels. Why?

## Barriers to evaluation

There are at least four barriers to the effective evaluation of PR:

- Cost
- Confusion
- Containment
- PR's paymasters making up their own minds

*Cost*: When PR is used as a part of the marketing mix it is usually the cheapest of the communication disciplines. An advertising campaign for a national company may well cost millions of dollars or pounds, simply in terms of buying media space. Set against this the cost of evaluating advertising results may seem quite economical. The budgets for PR are much smaller, but the cost of evaluation is not. Rightly or wrongly many organizations prefer to rely on their judgment as to whether a PR campaign has worked, rather than spend half as much again on evaluation. Ironically, PR's perceived cost-effectiveness militates against its proper measurement.

*Confusion*: Another problem that PR confronts when used as part of a marketing communication mix is confusion. By this we mean the confusion that exists over what part of the mix achieved what. How important was the advertising, the sales promotion, the price cut, the training of the sales team, or indeed other circumstances beyond the company's control?

The best way to find out would be to conduct the campaign without PR to see what happens. Of course this cannot be done. Again there is an irony – few people would want to take the chance because most believe PR plays a vital role: they just find it hard to prove.

*Containment*: Containing bad news and keeping stories out of the media, or at least reducing the amount and tone of negative coverage, is one of PR's most vital roles. Indeed moderating bad coverage in a crisis situation is usually harder to achieve than getting positive coverage in good times. But how can such an achievement be measured? How can you say how much bad coverage there would have been but for PR, and how can you measure the effect the coverage, if it had appeared, would have had? The answer, of course, is that it cannot be assessed with any accuracy at all.

*PR's paymasters making their own minds up*: Senior managers and others can read newspapers, magazines, and online reports and watch television just as readily as PR people. As they do so they will quickly form their own views about the effectiveness or otherwise of the PR for which they are paying. Is their message getting across? Is bad news being successfully dealt with? While the assessment of the success of a typical advertising campaign has typically to await sales figures, instant judgments can be and are made about PR.

> According to PR firm Edelman's ninth Trust Barometer, people in the UK place more trust in TV news coverage and newspaper articles as sources of information than they do in conversations with friends and peers.[7] However, rather confusingly, they also say they trust media institutions about as much as they trust government and considerably less than they trust business or NGOs. Perhaps people trust the media they consume but not "media institutions" in general, meaning the media others consume! The public's relationship with the media often seems to be ambiguous.

In areas such as lobbying, where media relations may be only a small or nonexistent element of a campaign, evaluation is also fraught with difficulty. A lobbying campaign that seeks to change the law, or stop a law being changed, seems at first glance easy to assess. It either did or did not happen. However, a host of factors may cause a change of government policy and it is difficult to attribute it to the activities of an individual lobbyist or campaign – and next to impossible to prove it beyond doubt. Gauging the success of a lobbyist will probably always remain a matter of judgment.

## Trusting to judgment

A survey in the United Kingdom by Bell Pottinger and Henley Management College in 2004 of chief executives of top businesses found that the majority were convinced that PR was an important tool, but believed that it was not really possible to measure its true value.[8]

There are numerous examples where public relations has played a hugely important role in the success of an organization. The early successes of Google, Richard Branson's Virgin and Starbucks, all of which became mega brands, were achieved with minimal advertising and some great PR. More recently the rise of Facebook, or the prelaunch hysteria surrounding Apple's Iphone have been attributed in large part to PR. Similarly, the initial success of former UK Prime Minister Tony Blair and former US President Clinton can be attributed in part to professional PR. And Greenpeace, Amnesty, and PETA would be little-known pressure groups if they were not expert at PR.

PR sometimes works and sometimes works very well indeed, though why it works and how it works are moot points. This lack of clarity is not a problem unique to PR. A famous quote from the world of advertising, attributed to Lord Leverhulme, the founder of Unilever, could equally be applied to PR. "Fifty per cent of my advertising works. The trouble is that I don't know which fifty per cent."

This uncertainty manifests itself in the fact that 80% of new product launches – the vast majority of which will have benefited from lots of PR – end in early failure.[9] On the other hand there is the obvious truism that PR money, like advertising money, follows successful and popular products. Would such products, with less or no PR, have succeeded anyway?

Similarly, a visible PR campaign, or even the promise of one, may be enough to galvanize a salesforce or encourage a retailer to stock up and motivate key staff. In such cases PR's benefit may derive not from its direct influence on consumers but from the way it injects enthusiasm and effort into the selling of a product. The PR will have worked, but next perhaps as expected.

Proctor & Gamble, in common with a number of other large manufacturers of consumer goods, has been investing recently in "market mix modelling." This is a costly process, highly dependent on accurate data and reckoned by some to be only viable for companies spending $50 million or more annually on marketing. However, despite these limitations the results for PR do seem encouraging. P&G tested six brands across a range of categories. For three of the brands tested PR gave the highest return on investment (ROI) and came second on the other three. Not surprisingly P&G are said to be expanding the number of products tested.[10]

Practitioners are keen to tell people that PR cannot make a bad product good. What they are less keen to admit is that a good product can make PR easy. Changes in population, income, and other non-PR related factors are often the biggest drivers of economic and social change. Financial services deregulation led to the explosion in sales of financial products: PR just helped. Similarly, the market for hats in the sixties collapsed because of John F. Kennedy's reluctance to don headgear, the explosion in car ownership (hats and cars do not work together), and the growth of longer hair styles led by the Beatles. No amount of great PR or advertising could do much about it. And, while the campaigns to sell mobile phones may have succeeded, consumers also wanted mobiles and sales were going to grow anyway.

It is a salutary lesson for anyone trying to persuade people of the omnipotence of the persuasive industries that two of the biggest and most successful areas of economic activity – illegal drugs and pornography – are almost totally devoid of any PR, or indeed advertising, support, at least in any form that the PR or advertising industries would recognize.

There is also the contradictory evidence provided by big and successful companies which seem to spend little on PR or actually have a poor PR image. How does one explain Wal-Mart in the United States which, despite a poor image, still prospers (and is indeed infinitely larger than all the much-vaunted ethical retailers); or the clothing retailer Primark in the United Kingdom which spends next to nothing on PR but is booming? Most of the companies that are seen as brilliant at PR are quite small and, secondly, are challenger brands fighting the established corporate giants, something the media love. It seems many much-pilloried large companies have a "reputation" for providing affordable goods and services that people want.

According to studies such as those run by *Fortune Magazine* there appears to be a link between reputation and performance – though there are many who dispute even this. There is a chicken and the egg issue here. Does good performance lead to a good reputation or vice versa? There is also the question of the degree to which PR practitioners actually create reputation or just help communicate it. Given how few PR people sit in the boardroom, and that they seldom create the products and services which are the building blocks of reputation, it is much more likely to be the latter.

The worry for the PR industry is that if their paymasters work out more clearly what does – and does not – work, and why, there might be much less PR in the future. But if PR has difficulty proving its value to individual organizations, it seems to be on firmer ground when it comes to the economy as a whole. The two most dynamic economies in the west in recent years have been those of the US and the UK, both homes to very strong and influential PR industries. It is hard to imagine that hard-nosed business leaders, media savvy politicians, and heads of NGOs would have continued to increase their spend on PR if they did not find that it worked, even if they often have trouble proving its precise value.

So how does PR help the economy as a whole? Along with other persuasive communication techniques such as advertising and sales promotion, PR is said to aid competition by providing consumers with information and explaining choices, thereby helping to lower prices. It is the cry of the stallholder in today's vast and complex markets. Persuasive communication can educate consumers about new products and new forms of behavior. People needed to know not just that mobile phones were available and increasingly inexpensive but that they could be used for building relationships and having fun, not just for "duty" calls. PR, working on behalf of a myriad of individual organizations, can have the cumulative effect of increasing consumption and lubricating the economy, something of particular importance in times of rapid change.

One industry is particularly dependent on PR: the media. As discussed in Chapter 3, without PR there would not be enough content to fill the enormous array of media products available today. Advertising and subscriptions alone are insufficient to finance the number of journalists needed to fill all the white space and air-time. PR funds media choice.

However, while the case for PR's contribution to the economy is strong it is not always clear whether PR is an even or fair force. PR is sometimes used not to keep prices down but help maintain them. Luxury goods manufacturers spend vast sums seeking to add perceived value to their brands. Similarly, big brands have big PR budgets. That can make it hard for smaller companies to enter the market and be heard. And, perhaps most tellingly, PR for an organization is always biased. This might not be a problem if consumers can weigh the competing claims of different products or services, but consumers seldom have either the time or the inclination.

Like advertising, PR may make for a dynamic economy and promote consumption, but it does not necessarily promote equity. The marketplace for information and ideas, like nearly all other markets, is imperfect.

## PR and society

> The development of the publicity man is a clear sign that the facts of modern life do not spontaneously take a shape in which they can be known. They must be given a shape by somebody.
>
> Walter Lippmann[11]

If PR works for capitalism, it also works for NGOs, campaigning groups, and political parties of all complexions. Even capitalism's most vigorous critics will use PR to try to persuade people to support them and achieve their goals. Given the variety of people and organizations that use PR (even if they call it something different) it is hard to assess its impact on society. Indeed there are PR arms races, as competing groups build up their PR muscle (and sometimes, amid the resulting noise, cancel each other out). On the one hand PR is blamed for encouraging wasteful consumption. On the other it is what is used – along with other persuasive techniques – to encourage safer driving, electoral registration, charitable giving, church attendance, and many other activities which are generally seen as beneficial. PR is morally neutral. It is the messenger not the message.

Nor is the messenger necessarily effective. Changing behavior that is based on deeply held beliefs, or long standing habit, is notoriously difficult. By definition a belief cannot be attacked with reason, and is immune to the assault of evidence. Consequently much social PR ends up preaching to the converted but having little impact on those whose behavior it wishes to change. Certainly over time stigmas can develop against certain kinds of behavior, but this usually requires the backing of the law. It has taken decades of persuasion coupled with legal action to persuade people to give up smoking and to make them less likely to drink and drive. Antidrug messages have been famously ineffective. Similarly, racial and sexual discrimination would surely still be openly practiced were it not for legislative action. Some PR advocates would claim that legislative action is the result of successful PR and lobbying. Critics would argue that legislation is necessary because PR on its own is not effective.

The reality is that PR is not as powerful as – paradoxically – both its advocates and detractors like to assert. The notion, popular among some critics, of an omnipotent PR industry, is one that provokes private smiles among senior PR people.

## The marketplace of ideas

Modern societies are loud argumentative marketplaces filled with goods, services, and ideas. As we have already noted, some of the stallholders in the market have more resources and a louder voice than others. This is not the fault of PR but a reflection of a range of inequalities in society (some of which are attacked and challenged using PR techniques). Moloney, in his thoughtful but ultimately rather naive book *Rethinking Public Relations*, argues that what he calls "communicative equality" can be achieved by establishing a kind of trust into which the "PR rich" would pay funds for use by the "PR poor," such as pensioners, immigrants, and the disabled.[12]

Aside from the issue of determining who contributed to and who benefited from such a trust – the decision of a committee of the gods would be challenged – Moloney fails to take into account that the media's and the public's natural sympathy and preference is for the underdog. Defending big business and the rich and powerful does not sell papers, nor does it usually go down well at the dinner tables of anyone other than the rich and powerful. The PR playing field may not be level, but it is bumpy and does not have an even gradient in any one direction.

Moloney refers to Parsons' belief that PR can be a force for good provided it follows her five key values.[13] These are:

1. Veracity (telling the truth)
2. Nonmalfeasance (doing no harm)
3. Beneficence (doing good)
4. Confidentiality (respecting privacy)
5. Fairness (social responsibility)

These sound, at first hearing, reasonable. However under examination they fall apart one by one. As we saw in Chapter 4, the truth is necessarily partial. Agreeing on definitions of malfeasance and beneficence is nigh on impossible. For example one person's well-meaning attempt to get the issue of immigration discussed will be seen by another as stirring up racial antagonisms which might ultimately lead to street violence. Confidentiality can come in to conflict with other priorities such as public interest. And notions of fairness are hard to define for a legal profession with many hundreds of years of experience, let alone a newer industry which seeks to represent opposite sides in the same argument without the formal structures and rules of the legal system. These ideas may be well-intentioned but lead nowhere.

## PR and mediated society

Many authors have worried about the effect of PR on media independence and objectivity. Moloney argues that in an ideal world PR would provide advocacy for interests and ideas and journalism would scrutinize them. In an imperfect way that is what happens, albeit with more PR people participating than journalists.[14] The media's desperate hunger for content means that the power – with the exception of some powerful titles and programs – has often passed to PR. But PR is not monolithic: a range of competing views is still reflected. Ideally, according to Moloney, journalists should treat PR people with a skepticism bordering on hostility.[15] Failure to do so endangers the notion of the independence of the media, which cannot be good for the effectiveness of PR in the long term.

At least journalists seeking to find "the truth," or put a brake on the corrupt or overly powerful, now have the Internet to help them. Digital records are hard to destroy. The dissatisfied and dispossessed can act collectively, quickly, and often effectively, exploiting the Internet in ways that were not hitherto possible. Journalists may have less time for investigative journalism but the Internet has made some aspects of investigation easier. Dishonest and misleading PR has become more difficult and more risky in the online world.

Nonetheless it is understandable that people are concerned about the increasing reliance of the media on PR. Subtract PR from society and people would lose vital information about politics, entertainment, shopping, business and so forth. But the tendency of some branches of PR to downplay the rational and play-up the emotional may lead to illogical no-go areas for science, while the obsession with celebrity, to which PR contributes, can lead to the rejection of the thoughtful and considered argument. The paradox remains that to tackle those threats people will have to employ PR.

Ironing out inequalities and strengthening the voice of reason are fine aspirations but it is difficult to envisage how such things could be done practically without undermining fundamental freedoms, creating bureaucratic and regulatory monstrosities and further distorting the marketplace.

## PR: a social good?

So is PR good for society? It is a little like asking if food is good for people. It is notable that within their borders dictators have no need for PR as they exert direct control over communication, while PR thrives and grows in democracies where freedom of speech is highly prized. PR is the babble of competing voices making their case and arguing their point. But to continue with the food analogy, too much of certain kinds of PR may be unhealthy. A balanced diet and the exercise of healthy skepticism are desirable. Few would doubt the importance of a healthy and independent media to the body of democracy and the sinews of free enterprise.

A parting thought. Much of the negative talk about PR is western and insular: a luxurious by-product of wealth and assured freedom. In many parts of the world, including most emerging democracies, PR not only surges ahead but is inseparably linked to rising prosperity, increased choice, and freedom of expression.

# CHAPTER 14

# The future of PR

Where is PR heading? Is it, as advertising appears to have done already, reaching maturity and now heading for a middle age of declining health and whingeing? Will the critics of PR have their day and mount an effective backlash? Or will PR continue to grow, particularly in the new democracies and developing world? And if it does continue to grow, will it follow the currently dominant Anglo-Saxon model or take off in a new direction?

We believe there are four main drivers of PR growth today:

*Globalization*: Once upon a time most sellers knew or could at least communicate directly with buyers. Change, including the industrial revolution and expanding distances and volumes of trade, made this impossible. Mass communication through the media helped overcome this problem. Now, with international markets and billions of consumers, mass global communications are necessary – although the old Unilever motto, think globally, act locally, still seems to hold good. Looking ahead it is hard to imagine any serious economy or company that does not make some use of the art of public relations.

*Reduced state ownership*: What began with Reagan and Thatcher in the 1980s has cascaded around the world as governments eschewed state ownership. As the Berlin Wall came down more and more countries decided that the state was an inefficient provider of goods and services. State assets were sold off. Modern management and marketing techniques were brought in. Those government departments and agencies that remain have to be more customer-focused and demonstrate value for money. This is good news for PR. State-owned monopolies have a limited need to communicate but the fates of competitive privately owned businesses are determined by their ability to communicate with different audiences. Similarly government departments and agencies which need to justify their existence spend increasing amounts of tax payers' money communicating. It is extremely unlikely that any major country will return to state ownership and centralized planning. The market economy – and its handmaiden PR – seems to be here to stay.

*The Internet and 24/7 news*: Organizations have never been under so much scrutiny. In the past angry customers could be isolated if not ignored, but today angry customers can band together quickly online and, if they so desire, seek change or try to destroy you. Similarly, rolling news and a general explosion in media channels means that there are more opportunities to proactively communicate your point of view (and be attacked) than ever before. All of this is good for PR. Even as print media sales decline new forms of digital media are emerging, requiring the skills of the PR practitioner. And more media, greater fragmentation, and greater audience segmentation means more work for more PR people if organizations want to communicate their messages.

*The death of political philosophies and the rise of single issues*: As we noted earlier, with the triumph of free market thinking, voters are finding fewer and fewer distinctions between different political parties, even those which are, or were, nominally socialist. Instead their interest and support is turning to single issues such as the environment, world poverty, animal rights, and equal opportunities. Each of these causes has a profusion of groups trying to persuade people not only to support the cause, but to support them rather than a rival group. This demands a lot of PR activity.

So what could hold PR back? The enemies of PR would seem to be state ownership, import tariffs (restricting global trade), and media censorship. At the time of writing the worldwide trend – with some obvious exceptions – is positive for PR.

It is worth considering why PR is more important in Anglo-Saxon cultures than, for example, in the capitalist economies of continental Europe or Japan. It is an area which requires more research. Of course PR – unconsciously and in other guises – has always been practiced in such societies, and there is some catching-up to do with what, in historic terms, is a relatively new American invention. However in considering the prominent role of PR in the English-speaking world the following factors bear examination:

- Anglo-Saxon *commercial culture* is particularly vigorous and competitive – or, in the eyes of critics, ruthless. The emergence of PR in its modern form coincided with antitrust legislation in the United States, which sought to break up monopolies. In the United Kingdom the boom in PR is associated with the free market reforms of the Thatcher era. PR can be seen as meeting a business need to be assertive and to maximize competitive advantage by making oneself heard and defend oneself in the marketplace. The huge financial markets – New York, London – of the Anglo-Saxon world place a particular onus on PR as they respond instantly to information and opinion. Other countries have moved in this direction, but more hesitantly. They often have traditions of a more consensual approach to business, and Anglo-Saxon capitalism (with PR as one of its weapon systems) is viewed with some trepidation or even repugnance. However, the current evidence in places as far apart as China and France is of a move towards the Anglo-Saxon model, or at least a finessed version thereof.

- The United States and the United Kingdom have long *traditions of press freedom*. This means that everyone – even powerful politicians and business leaders – has to live with a nagging anxiety about what might be said about them in the media, and cannot be certain of being able to say what they want via the media either. PR is an attempt to deal with this uncertainty. In many countries the tradition of media freedom is less well-established, and the media have a tradition of pulling their punches when it comes to discussing large companies and political leaders. Again there are signs of the media becoming freer and less passive, even in countries such as China. Moreover, fresh forms of news media – from radio and television, to digital media such as blogs – have inherited much of this more confident and combative tradition.

The private life of the late French President Mitterrand only became public knowledge in France via the media following his death in 1996, although there is no suggestion that the media – and indeed rival politicians – were previously unaware of the facts or unable to substantiate them.

Although Mitterrand's activities involved the misuse of public funds and were undoubtedly of public interest, the French media chose not to publicize the details. This reluctance to attack the powerful, which now shows signs of changing, would be unthinkable in many Anglo-Saxon democracies. It has meant that, traditionally, French politicians did not require the same heavy-armor plating of spin that has become familiar in the United States and United Kingdom.

Extensive coverage of the private life of the current French President, Nicolas Sarkozy, shows how much the situation has altered.

- The vigilance of the media may be imperfect but is backed up by *opposition parties, and by powerful pressure groups* that campaign on a wide range of issues. Although these are by no means unique to the Anglo-Saxon world, the tradition is stronger in north-west Europe than in the south or east of the continent. Not only are such pressure groups great users of PR resources themselves and a source of a large proportion of the material used by the news media, but they also compel the business world to deploy PR resources to counter their campaigns. There are no signs of this abating. Indeed it seems likely that as wealth and education grow, often leading to demands for democracy and reform, so too will the call for PR.

- The United States and the United Kingdom are *well-established democracies,* familiar with the clash of ideas in public. This clash takes place via the media and is facilitated by PR people. Although this may be true today for many other countries, it takes time to develop the deeper traditions of democracy. When countries emerge from dictatorships a stigma may be attached to any form of persuasion as it is associated with the propaganda of the past regime. Thus it has been argued that Germany's experience of Nazi propaganda retarded the growth of PR in the postwar federal republic, as did communism in East Germany. It is notable that Germany now has the biggest PR industry in mainland Europe.

## The future for PR

We believe that the PR consultancy market in the United States and United Kingdom is now mature. That is not to say that there will not be changes but that the range and nature of specialist provision will not change dramatically over the next decade. Certainly there will be claims to the contrary and there will be new firms claiming to specialize in CSR – *Corporate Social Responsibility.*

CSR refers to the increasingly popular idea in affluent democracies that businesses should not just make a profit but should exercise a range of social and environmental responsibilities – to their employees, suppliers, local communities, and wider society – and must not only act on these concerns but be seen to act in an accountable way. PR people often claim to play a key role in CSR. In the United States it is a core part of PR briefs and nearly all major PR consultancies now claim to offer CSR either as essential part of their activity or as a discrete service.

CSR is a new name – designed to attract more fees and claim a place in the boardroom – for what is an old practice. Well-run businesses that are concerned about their reputation have always responded to public, government, and NGO pressure to improve the quality of life. They have at times led by example. In fact there is a danger that PR's claim to own CSR may, given public cynicism about PR, undermine the credibility of some genuinely positive moves by corporations.

We predict that in a few years' time CSR will be less talked about. This will not be because moves to achieve corporate good citizenship have ceased, but because companies will have realized that trying to ghettoize it is counterproductive and creates suspicions. It will also be because they will have come to mistrust PR people who claim to be specialists in CSR, an area of activity that meets none of the criteria we identified in Chapter 5.

So-called *digital PR* firms are a more recent band of newcomers. The name is confusing as it refers to neither an audience nor an aspect of PR but a specific communication channel: "digital media." It is an example of PR firms seeking competitive advantage by surfing a trend. In our view this will be short-lived. Digital media are vitally important, but, once the main PR consultancies and consumers have grown accustomed to them, claiming to be "digital" will be redundant. There are, after all, hardly any PR consultancies devoted to other media categories, be they TV or print.

As for *internal communications*, we do not believe that the subdiscipline will be significant as Harold Burson claims (see Chapter 10) as it does not share the characteristics outlined in Chapter 5. People in PR have predicted for the last 25 years that internal communications is going to be the next big thing, so a little cynicism is appropriate. Internal PR is a major force which is here to stay but, other than in emerging economies where modern employment practices are still being learnt, there is unlikely to be a great expansion in its practice.

Some have argued that with the growth in regulation and NGO pressure, *lobbying* will become a mainstream PR skill. It is true that generalists will have to develop a better understanding of the political process. However, the obsessive nature of the political world and the peculiarities of political "animals," together with the importance of tactics other than media relations, mean that lobbying will remain a separate, powerful, but, outside a few centers of power, relatively small discipline. An obsession with politics does not sit comfortably with the mindset of the cynical dilettantes who populate mainstream PR!

Moreover for as long as capitalism and the financial and equity markets survive there will be *financial specialists*. The benefit of financial PR probably resides less in the value it adds than in the value that could be lost if communication goes wrong.

### Name games

People will continue to bandy about different names for PR, but they will find that the alternatives lack clarity and brand recognition. It is striking that the new marketing services conglomerates continue to use the term – for sound business reasons. Playing linguistic games will not put to rest the anxieties some have. A replacement for the term only changes the wrapping paper, and in any case the term PR is now thoroughly institutionalized across a plethora of PR trade associations, publications, and training courses.

## Areas of growth

So if the United States and the United Kingdom are mature markets where will the growth be? According to the ICCO (International Communications Consultancy Organization),[1] agency heads around the world see Central and Eastern Europe, Asia, and the Middle East as the clear winners. In terms of sectors they predict healthcare to be the specialization with the best growth potential followed by finance, then the public sector and IT, as these markets catch up. This sounds correct to us.

The cry from PR firms from all over the world is that there is a single major obstacle to growth: recruitment. They cannot get enough good people fast enough.[2] This can only mean one thing: more PR courses, more PR training, more PR books, more journalists jumping ship for PR, and no restricted entry any time soon.

# CHAPTER 15

# In defence of PR

Throughout this book we have pointed to a range of problems that beset the PR industry. Many of the wounds are self-inflicted and therefore needless. PR for PR – the one area where the industry is in undoubted control of the purpose and not just the message – has not been a triumph. Before we are accused of being negative we want to make a stalwart defence of public relations (or whatever it chooses to call itself now or in the future!).

There is a compelling pragmatic case for the public relations industry. It reflects the natural instinct of human beings and human organizations to promote themselves, the products and services they produce, and the arguments in which they believe. This reality cannot be curbed: it has existed and will exist in all societies. PR takes the current form we all know because of the nature of our societies and our mass media. Change those conditions and the nature of PR will change, but PR in some form will remain. Any attempt to control PR would not only involve thwarting those basic human instincts, but, as we have seen, would encounter enormous practical difficulties: imagine trying to regulate thousands of private conversations! The attempt at a cure would certainly be worse than any disease, which is why in their wisdom most legislatures allow PR to continue untrammeled.

But we contend that the case for PR is not merely pragmatic. PR is not just a regrettable fact of life, but a wholly legitimate aid to the exchange of information and ideas in society. Just as people are free to express themselves, they are also free to seek advice and assistance on how best to put their ideas across, and this includes consulting PR practitioners. Only conspiracy theorists would see this as necessarily sinister. Past writers have pointed to positive advantages that can accrue from the supply of PR material. Bernays observed that economic life in consumer societies would become hopelessly

jammed for people seeking to make choices were it not for the assistance of PR,[1] while from his vantage point as someone who had served
Britain's postwar Labour government, the historian of PR J. A. R.
Pimlott described how PR people play an essential role in bridging
the gap between ruler and ruled:

> They contribute to the smooth ordering of society by
> helping to disseminate that minimum of information
> without which the individual will be unable to play his
> part as a citizen, economic unit and neighbour.

For Pimlott public relations was one of the methods by which society adjusts to changing circumstances and resolves its clashes.[2]

The right to persuade is inseparable from democracy and the
working of a free market. What then is the problem? Is it that PR is
not a neutral purveyor of information and is involved in acts of persuasion which people will always view with suspicion? But to say
people must not be persuaded by means that may include the use of
PR is to belittle and demean them. Critics of PR seem to feel that *they*
can exercise due skepticism but adopt, perhaps unconsciously, a
patronizing attitude to others who they feel lack their powers of
perspicacity.

The crucial issue is not persuasion *per se* but the context in which
it takes place. Are others free to persuade? If so, all is well and good.
In our society it is a commonplace among what remains of the political left to deplore the persuasive propaganda work of large corporations, but for many people working for those corporations the
propaganda power of campaigning NGOs is even more of an issue:
the important thing is that all "sides" can, if they wish, put their
views across. Meanwhile political parties of all hues advance their
views. The ingenuity with which everyone does so is up to them.

Why are the official bodies and spokespeople of the PR industry
so reluctant to advance these arguments for PR? One reason that
keeps cropping up is a knee-jerk attempt to dissociate PR from anything unpleasant: if a cause or even the act of persuasion appears
unsavory then they attempt to say PR has nothing to do with it. This
is a misguided and counterproductive defence.

But deeper currents are swirling around. We cheerfully accept the
free market but have contended in this book that business is fundamentally amoral. For others this harsh reality is hard to stomach. Is

it possible that after experiencing the painful and sometimes humiliating abandonment of their socialist beliefs, including ideas of state-ownership of business, some of those thinking or writing about the subject seek a way out through PR? In the new world in which they now find themselves they desperately want to believe in the morality of business and hope they can play a part in this: hence the undue emphasis on Corporate Social Responsibility in some PR circles. However when they use CSR to try to give PR a veneer of morality they never explain why PR should be the singular possessor of a moral compass or why PR practitioners are particularly well placed to advise on what is responsible (as opposed to popular, or how things will play with the media, arenas where they have some expertise).

The reality is that PR as a discipline, whether used in business or elsewhere, is, like business, amoral – neither necessarily good nor bad. Many of those who write about PR are troubled by this. Industries buffeted by the swings and roundabouts of public opinion are particularly likely to turn to the ministrations of PR and such PR work is high-profile and controversial. PR people feel particularly exposed and can never duck moral responsibility as mere technicians: they are forever in the unforgivable position of Dr Goebbels, not Dr Werner von Braun, the Nazi rocket scientist who was able successfully to transfer his skills to the services of the American government. Legal representation of the odious does not attract odium in itself, but PR representation does.

A false claim to morality is worse than no claim at all: no-one likes hypocrisy. But even honest attempts to assert the moral high ground appear so far at odds with reality that they invite mockery. PR can in the end only contribute to the debate and the flow of information, not act as the umpire. PR people should not claim to be anything other than partial. The task of acting as PR's moral arbiter falls in the main to journalists. If journalists are at times inept, lazy, gullible, susceptible to pressure, succumb to herd instinct, or act as purveyors of entertainment rather than as dogged guardians of the truth they should blame themselves, not PR. The great *causes celebres* of media manipulation have all depended on journalists abandoning the high ground from which they so often pontificate.

There is a further problem with the po-faced defence of PR. It fails to do justice to what makes PR an exciting and interesting industry in the first place. PR jobs are plentiful and well-paid because

PR people are valued by organizations in all walks of life. Media relations may not seem grand enough for some sanctimonious individuals who only wish to discuss strategy, but it can be exhilarating. It is no accident that the highest-profile PR people have all been directly involved in such work. PR work is packed with human interest and offers great scope to display creativity. Above all, the chance to be a dilettante, to suck the best and most topical out of all kinds of organizations and omit much of the banal and routine, are enormously attractive facets of PR which remain difficult to own up to.

It would be a mistake to see PR as over-preoccupied with its problems. They certainly have not inhibited the industry's successful growth. To the extent to which they are legitimate concerns they reflect growing pains and a natural desire for respect. These are exacerbated by the nature of media comment. PR's relationship with journalism will forever be marked with tensions. Journalists will always prize ideals of independence, objectivity, and truth, and rightly so. The ideals may be imperfectly realized but are different from the forces which animate PR, an activity which, as we have said, seeks to further the objectives of its sponsors, and is rightly seen as guilty of cant when it claims otherwise. This creates a natural and perfectly healthy clash of interests.

Although most PR people get on cheerfully with their work, the industry can seem defensive and unable to tell the world more about itself. PR may attract a welter of comments from the wider public, but there are few places to turn for a balanced account. This book is an attempt to deal with this, to explain what PR is and what it does in realistic terms, even if that involves shattering some shibboleths. We only hope it provokes debate and further study and research.

Without PR the modern media would collapse. Without PR politicians would be ignorant of the needs and desires of their citizens, and people would be unaware of much of what government can do for them. Without PR consumers would have less information and choice, and companies would find it hard to respond to their customers. Without PR new ideas, new causes, and new ways of thinking would find it all but impossible to emerge. PR is central to freedom of speech in a modern democracy. Love it or loathe it, PR is here to stay. Even those who profess to loathe it had better know more about it.

# Notes

## Acknowledgments

*Websites were accessed on 29 March 2008 unless otherwise indicated. Details of films and television programmes cited are in the bibliography.*

1. "Confronting PR's moral obfuscations," Vol. 2, No. 2, 2005, pp. 18–24; "I'm a liar – and so are you: reflections on the aftermath of famous PR victory," Vol. 4, No. 1/2, 2007, pp. 5–7.
2. "PR: an infant learning to walk in the groves of academe?," No. 34, Autumn 2003, pp. 12–13.
3. *LISA e-journal*, Vol. IV, No.3, 2006, http://www.unicaen.fr/mrsh/lisa/publications/012/15goldsworthy.pdf.
4. *Symbolism: An International Journal of Critical Aesthetics*, propaganda topics, Renée Dickason (ed.), AMS Press Inc., forthcoming.

## 1  The allure of PR

1. See for example the UK Graduate Careers Survey 2003, http://www.ipr.org.uk/news/index.htm, accessed July 14, 2004.
2. http://www.china-embassy.org/eng/gyzg/t259626.htm.
3. http://www.prweek.com/uk/search/article/579012/Feature-Reach-new-Europe/.
4. http://www.ipra.org/archivefrontlinedetail.asp?issue=October+2006&articleid=233.
5. www.bls.gov/oco/content/ocos086.stm
6. http://www.cipr.co.uk/direct/news.asp?v1=factfile.
7. http://www.echoresearch.com/en/imageofpr/.
8. http://www.carma.com/research/CARMA%20Executive%20Summary%20-%20State%20of%20the%20PR%20Industry%202005.pdf.
9. Coombs, W. Timothy and Holladay, Sherry, J. *It's not Just PR: Public Relations in Society* (Blackwell, 2007) p. 8.
10. *Absolutely Fabulous*, Series 4, BBC Worldwide DVD 2002, commentary by Jon Plowman.
11. *Ibid.*
12. See remarks by Jon Aarons, IPR President at the IPR Careers Day, November 28, 2002. www.ipr.org.uk/news/speeches/Aarons-careers02.htm, accessed April 9, 2003.
13. http://books.guardian.co.uk/reviews/generalfiction/0,,631158,00.html.
14. He, Yujie, *Public Relations in China*, University of Westminster MA Thesis, 2002.
15. *Absolutely Fabulous*, Series 1, "Fashion."

16. See for example http://www.dailymail.co.uk/pages/live/femail/article.html? in_article_id=495503&in_page_id=1879.
17. Waugh, Daisy, *The New You Survival Kit: An Essential Guide to Etiquette, Rites and Customs among the Modern Elite* (London: Harper Collins, 2002) p. 17.
18. *Ibid.*, p. 8.
19. Episode 2.
20. *Four's A Crowd*. Warner Brothers, 1938, dir. Michael Curtiz, 91 min.
21. Bernays, Edward L., *Propaganda* (Horace Liveright, 1928) p. 9.
22. Ross, Irwin, *The Image Merchants: The Fabulous World of American Public Relations* (Weidenfeld & Nicolson, 1960) p. 14.
23. http://ipr.org.uk/news/stories/192.htm, accessed July 14, 2004.
24. The Advertising Association estimates that fewer than 20,000 people are employed in advertising agencies, although clearly more people earn their livelihood from advertising: http://www.adassoc.org.uk/Getting_into_advertising.pdf.

## 2 Girls, gurus, gays, and diversity

1. http://toughsledding.wordpress.com/2006/11/13/diversity-in-public-relations-could-use-a-fresh-perspective-from-men, accessed October 14, 2007.
2. *Ibid.*
3. www.prweek.com/uk/search/article/526847//
4. www.prweek.com/us/search/article/731287/French-evolution/ accessed August 19, 2007.
5. According to an IPR survey 83% of those on PR courses at UK universities were female, rising to 92% at postgraduate level: http://www.ipr.org.uk/news/stories/192.htm, accessed May 8, 2004.
6. http://toughsledding.wordpress.com/2006/11/13/diversity-in-public-relations-could-use-a-fresh-perspective-from-men, accessed October 14, 2007.
7. Williams, Bill (Management Books, 2000).
8. Haymarket Professional Publications Ltd.
9. *PR Week*/Bloom, Gross and Associates Salary Survey, published February 26, 2007.
10. Text100 survey 2001, www.prweek.com/us/search/article/115309//
11. www.women-in-pr.org/html/survey.html, conducted by Sharp End Infoseek, June 2002.
12. www.autismresearchcentre.com/docs/papers/2001_Connellan_etal.pdf.
13. Gray, John (Harper Collins, 1993).
14. PRCA report, PR Week UK, November 9, 2007.
15. Christina Odone, *New Statesman*, November 15, 1999, London.
16. Elizabeth Albrycht quoted on http://prstudies.typepad.com/weblog/2004/01/index.html.
17. http://psychology.ucdavis.edu/rainbow/html/facts_mental_health.html.
18. TM, when CEO of a major consultancy in the early 1990s, was asked by a client if he thought that a gay male member of his staff was suited to work on the client's traditionally masculine product. The client had never complained about the rest of the team – who were all women.
19. www.prweek.com/uk/search/article/526847//

20. www.prweek.com/us/search/article/115309//
21. http://www.prweek.com/uk/search/article/789078/OPINION-Industry-needs-reflect-social-diversity/

## 3 PR and the media

1. All-powerful newspaper columnist J. J. Hunsecker in the film *The Sweet Smell of Success*, when challenged about his reliance on press agents.
2. For the history of PR see, for example, Cutlip, Scott, *The Unseen Power: Public Relations, a History* (Lawrence Erlbaum Associates, 1994).
3. Davies, Nick, *Flat Earth News: An Award-winning Reporter Exposes Falsehood, Distortion and Propaganda in the Global Media* (Chatto and Windus, 2008) p. 52.
4. *Ibid.*, p. 63.
5. *Ibid.*, p. 97.
6. *Ibid.*, p. 85.
7. An exception is Aeron Davies' *Public Relations Democracy: Public Relations, Politics and the Mass Media in Britain* (Manchester University Press, 2002).
8. http://www.bryanappleyard.com/article.php?page=8&article_id=39.
9. *The Independent*, April 6, 2006.
10. Jackall, Robert and Hirota, Janice M., *Image Makers: Advertising, Public Relations, and the Ethos of Advocacy* (University of Chicago Press, 2000) p. 24.
11. See, for example, Brian McNair's *An Introduction to Political Communication* (Routledge, 1995) p. 65.
12. Moloney, Kevin, *Rethinking Public Relations: PR, Propaganda and Democracy* (Routledge, 2006) p. 13.
13. Hargreaves, Ian, *Journalism: Truth or Dare* (Oxford University Press, 2003) p. 181.
14. Max Clifford, *Daily Mail*, April 9, 2004.
15. Davies, Aeron, *op. cit.*, p. 179.
16. Moloney, *op. cit.*, p. 135.
17. Marr, Andrew, *My Trade: A Short History of British Journalism* (Macmillan, 2004) p. 112.
18. http://www.guardian.co.uk/france/story/0,,1230302,00.html.
19. Boorstin, Daniel J., *The Image or What Happened to the American Dream* (Penguin, 1962).
20. www.travellodge.co.uk.
21. Gregory, Martyn, *Dirty Tricks: British Airways' Secret War against Virgin Atlantic* (Warner Books, 1996) p. 33.
22. http://news.bbc.co.uk/1/hi/uk_politics/1823120.stm.
23. *The Daily Star*, April 7, 2004, p. 4.
24. http://news.bbc.co.uk/1/hi/uk/3621577.stm.
25. *Daily Mail*, April 7, 2004, p. 8 (and two more similar references).
26. *The Sun*, April 9, 2004, p. 12.
27. *Daily Mirror*, April 6, 2004, p. 4; *Daily Star*, April 7, 2004, p. 4; see also *Daily Mirror*, April 10, 2004, p. 56.
28. *Daily Mail*, April 5, 2004, p. 7; also appears in *The Daily Mirror*, April 6, 2004, p. 27.
29. *Sunday Telegraph*, April 11, 2004, p. 19.
30. *Ibid*.
31. *The Daily Telegraph*, April 8, 2004, p. 19.

32. *Daily Star*, April 7, 2004, p. 6.
33. *Daily Mirror*, April 10, 2004, p. 56.
34. *The Observer*, April 11, 2004, p. 18.
35. *The Sun*, April 10, 2004, p. 5.
36. *The Sunday Telegraph*, April 11, 2004, p. 19.
37. *Daily Mirror*, April 5, 2004, p. 4.
38. *The Times*, April 7, 2004, p. 18.
39. *The Mail on Sunday*, April 11, 2004, p. 16.
40. *The Sun*, April 10, 2004, p. 5.
41. *The Times*, April 5, 2004, p. 9.
42. *Mail on Sunday*, Night and Day Supplement, April 11, 2004, p. 4.
43. Davies, Nick, *op. cit.*, p. 3.
44. *Ibid.*, p. 397.

## 4   The lying game

1. Max Clifford, quoted in Moloney, *op.cit.*, p. 20.
2. Haines, Joe, *Glimmers of Twilight: Harold Wilson in Decline* (Politico's, 2004) p. 114.
3. Halliday, Stephen, *Underground to Everywhere: London's Underground in the Life of the Capital* (Sutton Publishing, 2001) p. 147.
4. *The Sweet Smell of Success.*
5. This section draws upon Simon Goldsworthy's article "I'm a liar – and so are you: reflections on the aftermath of famous PR victory," *Ethical Space: the International Journal of Communication Ethics*, Vol. 4, No. 1/2, 2007.
6. The result of this poll has never been published.
7. The author and journalist Phillip Knightley puts this into a contemporary context: "The military has a manual called Managing the Media at Wartime and one of the exhortations in that is never tell a lie unless you're certain the lie won't be discovered until the war is over." http://news.bbc.co.uk/1/hi/talking_point/forum/1604226.stm
8. Marr, *op. cit.*, 164.
9. http://news.bbc.co.uk/1/hi/programmes/newsnight/4973880.stm#hamster.
10. Quoted in L'Etang, Jacquie, and Pieczka, Magda (eds), *Critical Perspectives in Public Relations* (International Thomson Business Press, 1996) p. 49.
11. http://www.prweek.com/uk/search/article/233327//.
12. www.rm116.com/adcenter/files/bb_quotes.pdf.

## 5   Portrait of an industry

1. www.odwyerpr.com/pr_firm_rankings/independents.htm, accessed December 5, 2007.
2. Ewen, Stuart, *PR! A Social History of Spin* (Basic Books, 1996).
3. Miller, David and Dinan, William, "The rise of the PR industry in Britain 1979–1998," *European Journal of Communication*, Vol. 15, No. 1, March 2000, pp. 5–35.
4. One of the authors was approached by five different groups before selling his business. All the suitors were far more interested in his 30% plus margins than in strategic fit.
5. ICCO World Report Autumn 2006, available from www.iccopr.com.
6. Published April 20, 2007.

7. O'Dwyer, *op. cit.*
8. *Ibid.*
9. *PR Week* published April 20, 2007.
10. WKS, *Marketing Monitor* issue 3, 2007.
11. This account draws upon Karen S. Miller's *The Voice of Business: Hill & Knowlton and Postwar Public Relations* (University of North Carolina Press, 1999) and http://www.hillandknowlton.com/global/company/history, accessed July 9, 2004.
12. Prentice Hall Press, 1990.
13. En.wikipedia.org/wiki/Hill_&_Knowlton.
14. Ross, *op. cit.*, p. 252.
15. http://www.medianrecruit.co.uk/index.cfm?fa=contentGeneric.brbvikzqtqeomchq&pageId=261
16. Research by Centre for Economics and Business Research (CEBR).
17. According to research by UK-based PR search specialist Watson Helsby 85% of communications directors in the FTSE 100 (*Financial Times* top 100 quoted businesses) report directly to their CEOs.
18. http://www.prweek.com/uk/search/article/744086/Text100-looks-India-services/
19. Davies, Nick, *op. cit.*, p. 102.

## 6   The people in PR

1. Jackall and Hirota, *op. cit.*, p. 97.
2. Watson Helsby's Corporate Affairs Director Research Study, 2004.
3. US *PR Week*/Bloom Gross & Associates Salary Survey, 2007.
4. US Department of Labor, www.bls.gov/oco/content/ocos086.stm.
5. *PR Week* (UK) Salary Survey 2007/Objective Research.
6. Available from www.international-pr.eu.
7. *Profile*, May 16, 2001, IPR. The same edition was liberally adorned with photographs of Bell, leading us to conclude that the CIPR is destined to love him from afar.
8. Ross, *op. cit.*, p. 254.

## 7   From PR to propaganda

1. Wilcox, Dennis L., Ault, Phillip H., Agee, Warren K., and Cameron, Glen T., *Public Relations Strategies and Tactics* (Longman, 1999) p. 3.
2. Casuist is itself defined as "A person, esp. a theologian, who resolves cases of conscience, duty, etc.; a sophist, quibbler."
3. Harrison, Shirley, *Public Relations: An Introduction* (Routledge, 1995) p. 7.
4. Grunig, James E. and Hunt, Todd, *Managing Public Relations* (Holt, Rinehart and Winston, 1984) p. 22.
5. Cited in L'Etang and Pieczka, *op. cit.*, p. 31. Ross quotes an equivalent definition: public relations is "merely human decency which flows from a good heart," *op. cit.*, p. 15.
6. *Absolutely Fabulous*, Series 3, "Jealous."
7. http://www.guardian.co.uk/tv_and_radio/story/0,3604,1088095,00.html.
8. http://www.bbc.co.uk/radio4/today/reports/archive/interview/interview of the week transbenn.shtml.

9. Morgan, Piers, *The Insider: The Private Diaries of a Scandalous Decade* (Ebury Press, 2005) p. 458.

10. *PR Week* October 24, 2003.

11. Campbell, Alastair, *The Blair Years: Extracts from the Alastair Campbell Diaries* (Hutchinson, 2007).

12. Harrison, *op. cit.*, p. 10.

13. http://www.ipr.org.uk/unlockpr/Unlocking-Potential-Report.pdf, accessed July 27, 2004.

14. Ewen, *op. cit.*, p. 14.

15. Ross, *op. cit.*, p. 85.

16. For the history of propaganda, see Taylor, Philip M., *Munitions of the Mind: A History of Propaganda from the Ancient World to the Present Era* (Manchester University Press, 1995).

17. Century of the Self, http://www.bbc.co.uk/bbcfour/documentaries/features/century_of_the_self.shtml.

18. Originally described by Grunig and Hunt, *op. cit.*, but since developed in a range of books by James Grunig and others.

19. For example, pp. 8–12 of *The Public Relations Handbook* (ed. Theaker, Alison) (Routledge, 2001) is devoted to these models.

20. Welch, David, *The Third Reich: Politics and Propaganda* (Routledge, 1993) pp. 50–51. Any reader of Goebbels diaries will find they are replete with references to his studying the fruits of postal censorship, secret police reports, and primitive opinion research, the better to adapt the tone and content of his propaganda.

21. Taithe, Bertrand and Thornton, Tim (eds), *Propaganda, Political Rhetoric and Identity 1300–2000* (Sutton Publishing, 1999) p. 1.

22. For example, see http://www.ipr.org.uk/Membership/membership.htm, accessed May 25, 2006.

23. For example, Taylor, Fred (ed.), *The Goebbels Diaries* (Hamish Hamilton, 1982) pp. 361, 71.

24. Balfour, Michael, *Propaganda in War 1939–1945: Organizations, Policies and Publics in Britain and Germany* (Routledge and Kegan Paul, 1979) p. 428.

25. Cull, Nicholas John, *Selling War: The British Propaganda Campaign against American "Neutrality" in World War II* (Oxford University Press, 1995) p. xi.

26. Taylor, Philip M., *op. cit.*, p. 6. O'Shaughnessy has similarly identified rhetoric as a "sub-set" of propaganda in O'Shaughnessy, Nicholas Jackson, *Politics and Propaganda: Weapons of Mass Seduction* (Manchester University Press, 2004), p. 66.

27. Stauber, John and Rampton, Sheldon, *Toxic Sludge Is Good For You: Lies, Damn Lies and the Public Relations Industry* (Constable and Robinson, 2004) p. 22.

28. Ross, *op. cit.*, p. 114.

29. Stauber and Rampton, *op. cit.*, p. 24.

30. Manvell, Roger and Frankel, Heinrich, *Doctor Goebbels: His Life and Death* (Heinemann, 1960) p. 264.

## 8   Professional, but never a profession

1. Peter Gummer, now Lord Chadlington, founder of Shandwick, http://www.prwatch.org/prwissues/2000Q1/shandwick.html.

2. L'Etang, Jacquie, *Public Relations in Britain* (Laurence Erlbaum Associates, 2004) p. 98.

3. According to Theaker (ed.), *op. cit.*, p. 61, only 17 people are qualified to practice PR in Switzerland. This seems wildly implausible. It is also far from clear that attempts to regulate PR practice in Brazil have been successful (see Juan-Carlos Molleda and Andrea Athaydes, "Public relations licensing in Brazil: evolution and the views of professionals," *Public Relations Review*, Vol. 29, No. 3, September 2003).
4. L'Etang, Jacquie, *op. cit.*, pp. 184–185.
5. http://media.guardian.co.uk/marketingandpr/story/0,7494,580149,00.html.
6. http://www.prweek.com/uk/search/article/774390/Exposure-pays-Kidman-spat/
7. http://www.prsa.org/aboutUs/ethics/preamble_en.html.
8. http://www.prsa.org/aboutUs/ethics/documents/enforcement.pdf.
9. See, for example, "Law Society could lose power over solicitors as report condemns failures," http://www.guardian.co.uk/uk_news/story/0,,1254942,00.html.
10. http://www.gmcpressoffice.org.uk/apps/news/events/index.php?key=0.
11. See, for example, http://www.gmcpressoffice.org.uk/apps/news/events/. The Institute of Chartered Accountants also lists hearings on its website: http://www.icaew.co.uk/index.cfm?AUB=TB2I_47337,MNXI_47337&route=11295,P,11322,47337.
12. http://www.ipr.org.uk/direct/membership.asp?v1=code, accessed July 26, 2004.

## 9 PR in the not-for-profit sector

1. Blood, Robert, "Living in an NGO World," in Gregory, Anne (ed.), *PR in Practice* (Kogan Page 2003) pp. 186–199.
2. *Ibid.*, p. 186.
3. *Ibid.*, p. 187.
4. Davies, Nick, *op. cit.*, p. 41.
5. *Ibid.*, p. 190.

## 10 Internal communications

1. http://www.prweek.com/uk/search/article/520781/internal-comms-key-says-burson/
2. Bunting, Madeleine, *Willing Slaves: How the Overwork Culture is Ruling Our Lives* (Harper Collins, 2004) pp. 109 and 99.
3. http://www.prweek.com/uk/search/article/94936/platform-cruel-kind-increase-profits-want-achieve-effective-internal-communications-canrsquot-always-afford-mr-nice-guy-says-alan-riley/
4. Bunting, *op. cit.*, p. 103.

## 11 PR and academia

1. Tye, Larry, *The Father of Spin: Edward L. Bernays and the Birth of Public Relations* (Owl Books, New York) p. 232.
2. *Ibid.*, p. 216.
3. Morley, Michael, *How to Manage Your Global Reputation: A Guide to the Dynamics of International Public Relations* (Macmillan, 1998) p. 40.

4. Criteria and Procedures for IPR Recognition of Diploma and Degree Programmes in Public Relations, June 2000, p. 3.
5. http://publicsphere.typepad.com/behindthespin/2006/06/why_pr_degrees_.html

## 12    Lobbying, public affairs, politics, and government PR

1. http://www.washingtonpost.com/wp-dyn/content/article/2006/01/06/AR2006010602251.html
2. *New York Times*, Washington, April 28, 1992.
3. Ross, *op. cit.*, pp. 219 and 221.
4. http://www.guardian.co.uk/politics/2000/jun/07/uk.londonmayor
5. http://news.bbc.co.uk/1/hi/uk/128061.stm
6. Pitcher, George, *The Death of Spin* (John Wiley and Sons, 2003) p. 3.

## 13    Does PR work and is it good for us?

1. L'Etang, *op. cit.*, p. 161.
2. cohenpr.com/does_pr_work.htm.
3. Moloney, *op. cit.*, p. 67.
4. Theaker, *op. cit.*, p. 29.
5. www.usatoday.com/life/2003–05-27-media-trust_x.htm
6. Stauber and Rampton, *op. cit.*, p. 1.
7. *PR Week*, January 25, 2008.
8. www.insightmkt.com/ceo_pr_briefing/findings.asp.
9. Brierley, Sean, *The Advertising Handbook* (Routledge, 2005) p. 236.
10. https://event.on24.com/eventRegistration/EventLobbyServlet?target=registration.jsp&eventid=22888&sessionid=1&key=5EADC0E5569D4292EA2409878C6CB765&sourcepage=register (webcast).
11. Lippmann, Walter, *Public Opinion* (George Allen & Unwin, 1922) p. 345.
12. Moloney, *op. cit.*, pp. 79–83.
13. *Ibid.*, p. 104.
14. *Ibid.*, p. 162.
15. *Ibid.*, p. 164.

## 14    The future of PR

1. ICCO World Report Autumn 2006, www.iccopr.com.
2. The State of the Public Relations Industry 2007: Holmes Report. www.holmesreport.com.

## 15    In defence of PR

1. Bernays, *op. cit.*, p. 11.
2. Pimlott, J. A. R., *Public Relations and American Democracy* (Kennikat, 1972) pp. 239–243.

# Some suggested reading and sources of information

Bernays, Edward L., *Propaganda* (Horace Liveright, 1928)

Boorstin, Daniel J., *The Image, or What Happened to the American Dream* (Penguin, 1962)

Borkowski, Mark, *Improperganda: The Art of the Publicity Stunt* (Vision On, 2000)

Campbell, Alastair and Stott, Richard (ed.), *The Blair Years: Extracts from the Alastair Campbell Diaries* (Hutchinson, 2007)

Clifford, Max and Levin, Angela, *Max Clifford: Read All About It* (Virgin Books, 2005)

Coombs, W. Timothy and Holladay, Sherry J., *It's Not Just PR: Public Relations in Society* (Blackwell, 2007)

Cutlip, Scott M., *The Unseen Power: Public Relations. A History* (Lawrence Erlbaum, 1994)

Davies, Aeron, *Public Relations Democracy: Public Relations, Politics and the Mass Media in Britain* (Manchester University Press, 2002)

Davies, Nick, *Flat Earth News: An Award-winning Reporter Exposes Falsehood, Distortion and Propaganda in the Global Media* (Chatto & Windus, 2008)

Ewen, Stuart, *PR! A Social History of Spin* (Basic Books, 1996)

Fishkin, James S., *The Voice of the People: Public Opinion and Democracy* (Yale University Press, 1997)

Fombrun, Charles, *Reputation: Realizing Value from the Corporate Image* (Harvard Business School Press, 1996)

Franklin, Bob, *Packaging Politics: Political Communication in Britain's Media Democracy* (Arnold, 2004)

Gregory, Martyn, *Dirty Tricks: British Airways' Secret War Against Virgin Atlantic* (Warner, 1996)

Grunig, James E. (ed.), *Excellence in Public Relations and Communication Management* (Lawrence Erlbaum, 1992)

Grunig, James E. and Hunt, Todd, *Managing Public Relations* (Rinehart and Winston, 1984)

Hargreaves, Ian, *Journalism: Truth or Dare* (Oxford University Press, 2003)

Harrison, Shirley, *Public Relations: An Introduction* (Routledge, 1995, second edition published by Thomson Learning, 2000)

Hobsbawm, Julia (ed.), *Where The Truth Lies: Trust and Morality in PR and Journalism* (Atlantic, 2006)

Hollingsworth, Mark, *The Ultimate Spin Doctor: The Life and Fast Times of Tim Bell* (Coronet, 1997)

Jackall, Robert and Hirota, Janice M., *Image Makers: Advertising, Public Relations, and the Ethos of Advocacy* (University of Chicago Press, 2000)

John, Steven, *The Persuaders: When Lobbyists Matter* (Palgrave Macmillan, 2002)

Kitchen, Philip (ed.), *Public Relations: Principles and Practice* (Thomson Learning, 1997)

Kunczik, Michael, *Images of Nations and International Public Relations* (Lawrence Erlbaum, 1996)

Lippmann, Walter, *Public Opinion* (George Allen & Unwin, 1922)

L'Etang, Jacquie, *Public Relations in Britain: A History of Professional Practice in the 20th Century* (Lawrence Erlbaum Associates, 2004)

L'Etang, Jacquie and Piezcka, Magda (eds), *Critical Perspectives in Public Relations* (International Thomson Business Press, 1996)

Marchand, Roland, *Creating the Corporate Soul: The Rise of Public Relations and Corporate Imagery in American Big Business* (University of California Press, 1998)

Marr, Andrew, *My Trade: A Short History of British Journalism* (Macmillan, 2004)

McNair, Brian, *An Introduction to Political Communication* (Routledge, 2003)

Manning, Paul, *News and News Sources: A Critical Introduction* (Sage, 2001)

Michie, David, *The Invisible Persuaders: How Britain's Spin Doctors Manipulate the Media* (Bantam, 1998)

Miller, Charles, *Politico's Guide to Political Lobbying* (Politico's, 2000)

Moloney, Kevin, *Rethinking Public Relations: PR, Propaganda and Democracy* (Routledge, 2006)

Morley, Michael, *How to Manage Your Global Reputation: A Guide to the Dynamics of International Public Relations* (Macmillan 1998)

Miller, Karen S., *The Voice of Business: Hill & Knowlton and Postwar Public Relations* (University of North Carolina Press, 1999)

O'Shaughnessy, Nicholas J., *Politics and Propaganda: Weapons of Mass Seduction* (Manchester University Press, 2004)

Palast, Greg, *The Best Democracy Money Can Buy: An Investigative Reporter Exposes the Truth about Globalization, Corporate Cons and High Finance Fraudsters* (Pluto, 2002)

Pimlott, J.A.R., *Public Relations and American Democracy* (Kennikat, 1972; first published 1951)

Pitcher, George, *The Death of Spin* (John Wiley and Sons, 2003)

Pratkanis, Anthony R. and Aronson, Elliot, *Age of Propaganda: The Everyday Use and Abuse of Persuasion* (W H Freeman, 2001)

Ross, Irwin, *The Image Merchants: The Fabulous World of American Public Relations* (Weidenfeld & Nicolson, 1960)

Scammell, Margaret, *Designer Politics: How Elections Are Won* (Macmillan, 1995)

Schudson, Michael, *Advertising, the Uneasy Persuasion: Its Dubious Impact on American Society* (Basic Books, 1986)

Schudson, Michael, *Discovering the News: A Social History of American Newspapers* (Basic Books, 1978)

Stauber, John and Rampton, Sheldon, *Toxic Sludge Is Good For You: Lies, Damn Lies and the Public Relations Industry* (Constable & Robinson, 2004)

Stauber, John and Rampton, Sheldon, *Trust Us, We're Experts! How Industry Manipulates Science and Gambles Your Future* (Tarcher/Putnam, 2001)

Taylor, Philip, *Munitions of the Mind: A History of Propaganda from the Ancient World to the Present Era* (Manchester University Press, 1995)

Theaker, Alison (ed.), *The Public Relations Handbook* (Routledge, 2002)
Thompson, John B., *Political Scandal: Power and Visibility in the Media Age* (Polity, 2000)
Trento, Susan B., *The Power House: Robert Keith Gray and the Selling of Access and Influence in Washington* (St Martin's Press, 1992)
Tumber, Howard (ed.), *Media Power, Professionals and Policies* (Routledge, 2000)
Tye, Larry, *The Father of Spin: Edward L. Bernays and the Birth of Public Relations* (Owl Books, 2002)

## Novels

Buckley, Christopher, *Thank you for Smoking* (Allison and Busby, 2003)
Dezenhall, Eric, *Jackie Disaster* (Thomas Dunne, 2003)
Lancaster, Graham, *Grave Song* (Hodder and Stoughton, 1996)
Michie, David, *Conflict of Interest* (Little, Brown, 2000)
Price, Daniel, *Slick* (Villard, 2004)
Priestley, J.B., *The Image Men* (Mandarin, 1996)
Thebo, Mimi, *The Saint Who Loved Me* (Allison and Busby, 2002)
Torday, Paul, *Salmon Fishing in the Yemen,* (Weidenfeld and Nicholson, 2007)
Waugh, Daisy, *The New You Survival Kit* (Harper Collins, 2002)
Wilson, Sloan, *The Man in the Gray Flannel Suit* (Four Walls Eight Windows, 2002)

## Films and TV

*Absolutely Fabulous* http://www.bbc.co.uk/comedy/abfab/
*Absolute Power* http://www.bbc.co.uk/comedy/absolutepower/
*Bridget Jones' Diary* (Universal Studios, 2001, dir. Sharon Maguire, 132 min.)
*The Century of the Self* http://www.bbc.co.uk/bbcfour/documentaries/features/century_of_the_self.shtml
*The China Syndrome* (Colombia Pictures, 1979, dir. James Bridges, 117 min.)
*Days of Wine and Roses* (Warner Brothers, 1962, dir.Blake Edwards, 113 min.)
*Four's a Crowd* (Warner Brothers, 1938, dir. Michael Curtiz, 91 min.)
*The Man in a Gray Flannel Suit* (20th Century Fox, 1956, dir. Nunnally Johnson, 152 min.)
*Phonebooth* (20th Century Fox, 2002, dir. Joel Schumacher, 77 min.)
*PoweR Girls* http://www.mtv.com/ontv/dyn/power_girls/series.jhtml
*Primary Colors* (Award Entertainment, 1998, dir. Mike Nichols, 143 min.)
*Sex and the City* http://www.hbo.com/city/
*Sliding Doors* (Intermedia Films, 1998, dir. Peter Howitt, 99 min.)
*Spin City* http://www.tv.com/spin-city/show/220/summary.html
*The Sweet Smell of Success* (Metro Goldwyn Meyer, 1957, dir. Alexander Mackendrick, 93 min.)
*Thank You for Smoking* (Room 9 Entertainment, 2005, dir. Jason Reitman, 92 min.)
*The Thick of It* http://www.bbc.co.uk/comedy/thethickofit/index.shtml
*Wag the Dog* (Baltimore Pictures, 1997, dir. Barry Levinson, 97 min.)
*Waikiki Wedding* (Paramount, 1937, dir. Frank Tuttle, 89min.)

## Websites

### Trade organizations

www.amecorg.com Association of Media Evaluation Companies
www.cerp.org European Public Relations Confederation
www.cipr.co.uk Chartered Institute of Public Relations (UK)
www.iabc.com International Association of Business Communicators
www.iccopr.com International Communications Consultancy Organization
www.ipra.org International Public Relations Association
www.prca.org.uk Public Relations Consultants Association (UK)
www.prfirms.org Council of Public Relations Firms (US)
www.prsa.org Public Relations Society of America
www.warc.com World Advertising Research Center

### Trade websites and papers

www.holmesreport.com
www.odwyerpr.com
www.prweek.com

### Critical sites

www.prwatch.org
www.spinwatch.org
www.corpwatch.org

### Some examples of PR-related blogs and websites

http://www.edelman.com/speak_up/blog/
http://www.forimmediaterelease.biz/
http://www.globalprblogweek.com/
http://blogs.hillandknowlton.com/blogs/
http://holmesreport.blogspot.com/
http://www.thenewpr.com/wiki/pmwiki.php
http://prstudies.typepad.com/weblog/
www.strumpette.com

# About the authors

## Trevor Morris, FRSA

Trevor Morris is Visiting Professor in Public Relations at Westminster University and a business consultant and mentor. He was formerly the high profile CEO of Chime Public Relations, Britain's biggest PR group. *PR week* recently described him as "one of the most influential people in PR."

As an entrepreneurial businessman Trevor shaped and led the management buyout of QBO, a top UK PR consultancy, and then grew the business to achieve margins of over 30% before selling it to Chime plc in November 2000.

As a public relations consultant he led campaigns from crisis management to brand building and public information for blue chip commercial and government clients.

Former colleagues range from Lord Tim Bell (former Prime Minister Lady Thatcher's favorite PR man), David Hill (former Prime Minister Tony Blair's press advisor) and Rosie Boycott (journalist and broadcaster) through to Sophie Rhys-Jones (the Countess of Wessex, the wife of Prince Edward).

He organized and chaired the controversial PR Week and University of Westminster debate "PR has a duty to tell the truth" and took part in a follow-up debate on the same theme at the Sorbonne in Paris.

Trevor has a BA Combined Honours in History and Politics from Exeter and a Postgraduate Certificate in Education from the University of London. He has lectured at the University of Westminster, City University, Exeter University, the Sorbonne, and Richmond, the American International University.

Married with two daughters, Trevor lives in Battersea, South London. He is a regular theater goer, a keen reader of contemporary fiction, and lifelong supporter and season ticket holder of Fulham Football Club.

## Simon Goldsworthy

Simon Goldsworthy is Senior Lecturer in Public Communication at the University of Westminster.

He has a first class degree in History from the University of London, and was formerly a member of the UK's Government Information Service, undertaking press and publicity work for a range of government departments, including the Central Office of Information, the Department of Trade and Industry, the Department of Social Security and the Department of the Environment. His duties included advising of government ministers on media handling. He subsequently worked both independently and for a number of PR consultancies running PR projects for a wide range of public sector organizations, including an award winning web-based campaign for the UK's largest science research council.

In 2000 Simon launched the first MA program in Public Relations in London at the University of Westminster, adding an undergraduate program two years later. Both programs attract large numbers of students from all over the world, and benefit from excellent links with key figures in the PR industry, many of whom are guest speakers.

Simon has also set up and run courses for universities in other countries, including Johns Hopkins University in the USA, is *Professeur Invité, Chaire Duprond*, Université Paris-Sorbonne, and has acted as consultant and external examiner for a number of PR courses at other UK universities. He has also published a range of academic articles on subjects including PR education and ethics, the relationship between PR and advertising, and aspects of journalism.

Simon took part in the controversial PR Week and University of Westminster debate "PR has a duty to tell the truth," which provoked considerable interest in PR circles internationally, and argued the opposite case in a follow-up debate at the Sorbonne in Paris.

Simon lives in Chiswick, West London. He is a keen traveler, cinema-goer, and reader of history. He is married, with a young son who supports Chelsea Football Club.

# Index